MINISTERS OF YOUR JOY

JOSEPH RATZINGER

MINISTERS
OF YOUR JOY

Meditations on
priestly spirituality

 St Paul Publications

Original title: *Diener eurer Freude*
© Verlag Herder, Freiburg im Breisgau, 1988

Translated from the German by Robert Nowell

Cover design by Mary Lou Winters FSP

St Paul Publications
Middlegreen, Slough SL3 6BT, England

English translation copyright:
  © St Paul Publications, Slough, 1989 and
  Crossroad Publishing Co., New York, 1989

Printed byBilling and Sons, Worcester
ISBN 085439 287 4

St Paul Publications is an activity of the priests and brothers of the Society of St Paul who proclaim the Gospel through the media of social communication.

CONTENTS

FOREWORD

Of recent years I was often faced with the necessity of preaching on the priesthood at Masses in seminaries or for priests. Instead of continually looking back to the familiar New Testament texts on this subject for these occasions, it seemed to me more fruitful to let myself be challenged by the readings I was provided with by the liturgy of the day. When recently after some time had elapsed I read over the texts that had emerged in this way it struck me that this method was indeed fruitful: new approaches opened up, different perspectives became visible, and the thoughts that had been occasioned by a variety of causes fitted together to form an internal unity. This emboldened me to the venture of collecting some of these sermons together and offering them unaltered, as they were delivered, to a wider public. I hope they can serve not only a fresh inward acceptance of the priest's task but also become an aid to meditative reflection on Holy Scripture and thus convey to both priests and lay-people a new joy in the Bible.

Perhaps it would be helpful to the reader if I were to say something briefly about the place and time that each individual contribution originated. The first sermon printed here goes back a long way: it was delivered in 1962 – on Sexagesima Sunday, the Sunday ten days before the start of Lent in the old calendar – at a priest's first Mass in the Rhineland. By accident I came across the manuscript, which I had long forgotten about, just as I was mulling over a collection of this kind. I was surprised to see how completely it fitted into the train of thought of the other texts and how consistent my ideas had remained in this time of change. So it seemed the right thing to do to put this piece at the beginning. The second sermon was given on the Thirteenth Sunday of the Year (Cycle C) in 1986 at the four hundredth anniversary of the Bamberg seminary; the third a few days later at the Mass on the eve of the Feast of St John the Baptist for a gathering of priests from the diocese of Regensburg. The fourth and fifth sermons I gave on the Third Sunday of Easter in Toronto, again in 1986: the first in St Michael's College, the second in St Augustine's Seminary. The sixth homily finally took shape in 1984 for visits to the seminaries at Dallas and St Paul, Minnesota, in the United States.

Since this is a collection of meditations which as such do not make any claims to scholarship I have forsworn footnotes completely. The reader can easily perceive that for exegetical and historical information I have been guided by the available commentaries, especially *Das Neue Testament Deutsch* and the large Herder *Theologischer Kommentar zum Neuen Testament.* The last piece included here (pp. 95ff.) has a different character. It is the meditation occasioned by the golden jubilee of Cardinal Höffner's ordination to the priesthood, which appeared in 1983 as volume 9 of the new series of *Kölner Beiträge.* I have included it here because it makes clear the fundamental theological decisions that underpin the whole.

The theme that runs through all these reflections is the joy that comes from the gospel. I hope therefore that this slim volume may help to serve this joy and thereby answer the inmost meaning of the priest's task.

Rome, on the First Sunday of Lent, 1988

Joseph Cardinal Ratzinger

I

THERE ARE ALWAYS SEEDS THAT BEAR FRUIT FOR THE HARVEST

'A sower went out to sow...' (Lk 8:4-15)

The crowds were still thronging to Jesus when he preached the parable of the sower, but already the first shadows of disappointment and disillusionment must have spread over the group of his followers. For the parable can already talk about the unbelief of those who hear and yet do not hear, who see and yet do not see. It must already have become clear around this time that the people who still continually ran after the Lord in crowds were in reality discontented with him; that in reality they did not want him at all, the Messiah who preached and healed, who was kind to the poor and the weak and was himself one of these, but that they wanted for themselves something quite different – the hero who sounded the trumpet and put the enemy to flight, the miraculous king who was to provide Israel with a land of milk and honey, a paradise of unbounded affluence. It must already have been clear that most of those who followed him were only fellow-travellers without roots and without depth who would abandon him at the first approach of danger.

In contestation and discouragement

It is to this situation of the disciples' first disappointment and the start of their discouragement that the parable is addressed. For the disciples themselves, the Twelve whom the Lord had drawn closest to himself, could ask themselves: 'How is this to continue? What is to become of the achievement that exhausts itself in words and individual miracles? How is Israel's salvation to come about if all he does is to preach, to spin words, and here and there occasionally heal some person of no influence or significance; if the little flock of those who stand by him is continually being reduced, if he meets with failure in the form of a message that is rejected ever more clearly and in the form of increasing opposition among influential circles?'

In this situation of contestation, of approaching discouragement, Jesus points out to the sower through whose work comes the bread from which people live. Even his activity, this decisive activity on which people's lives depend, seems like a hopeless undertaking. There are far too many dangers opposed to the seed growing: the unworkable stony ground, the weeds, the bad weather – everything seems to condemn his work to failure. We need to think of the often almost hopeless situation of the peasant in Israel who gathers his harvest from a soil that at every moment threatens to revert to desert. And yet, however much is done in vain, there are always seeds that germinate and thrive for the harvest, that despite all perils grow to bear fruit and reward all the toil many times over.

What Jesus wants to say with this story is that all truly fruitful things begin in this world with what is small and hidden. And God himself conformed to this law with his work in the world. God himself entered this age incognito, in the form of wretchedness, of powerlessness. And the realities of God – truth, justice, love – are small and downtrodden realities in this world. Nevertheless it is from them that men and women live, that the world lives, and if they did not exist they could not survive. Yet they persist when what is noisy and throws its weight around has long since decayed and been forgotten. So with this parable Jesus wants to tell his disciples that the tiny thing that is beginning here in his preaching will go on growing when what today throws its weight around has long since foundered.

In fact if we look back today we must say that history has proved the Lord right. The great empires of that time have disappeared, their palaces and buildings covered by the dust of the desert. The famous and important people of that age have been forgotten or live on here and there as leading figures from the past in history books. But what happened in the unimportant corner of Galilee, what Jesus began with that small group of men, of insignificant fishermen, that has remained, that today is still a present reality – *his* words have not passed away, they have been proclaimed in all places of the earth until our own day. The word has ripened, despite all wretchedness and contrary to all the powers that by human foresight should have smothered it.

The sower of the word today

In the hour in which we are meeting the story of a sower is beginning once again. A young man has put himself at the Lord's disposal as a sower of the word. And so the Lord's parable, the word of encouragement, of hope and of joy, is told in this our time too.

We all know that today the faith is still contested, is indeed again being contested, with the aim of attacking and overcoming us, so that we ask: 'Isn't it all in vain? How is the wretched power of the faith to survive among the gigantic powers of this world? Must it not simply be crushed between the world powers of atheism, must it not simply give in before technology and science and all their potential and discoveries? Must it not simply capitulate before the egoism and the covetousness that have become overpowerful and can no longer be restrained?' And we might ask: 'Does it still make any sense today to become a priest, a sower of the word? Are there not for a young man more promising, more profitable and more successful occupations in which he can better develop his gifts?'

Isn't the whole thing then a hopelessly out-dated cause? Isn't the time past when the faithful hastened to church? Do you not see, we hear people say, how everything is slowly but surely crumbling away? How you are fighting a losing battle? In fact God is still continually moving incognito through history. He is still continually veiling his power in the garb of powerlessness. And still continually the true values, the divine values, truth, love, faith, justice, are the forgotten and powerless things in this world. And yet – this parable says: 'Be comforted!' God's harvest is growing: however much there are also fellow-travellers who run away as soon as this seems advisable; however much is done in vain, somewhere the word is ripening. Even today. Even today it is still not in vain that there are people who venture to proclaim the word and to be there for the sake of the word; who venture to resist the flood of selfishness, of covetousness, of unscrupulousness, and to build a dam against it. Somewhere in silence their seed is ripening. Nothing is in vain. Secretly the world lives from the fact that in it people are still continually believing, hoping and loving.

Of course, it can often enough seem that the priest, the sower of the word, is fighting a losing battle; that he is a failure, as we have learned from Paul in the epistle, telling us how he escaped from one hopeless impasse only to land in another. But just as this Paul in the middle of all the weakness and opposition he suffered was continually able to experience with happy astonishment the glorious goodness of God which in a really frightening series of catastrophes turned him into a man full of optimism, full of undaunted hope and full of joy, so too will the priest despite all kinds of disappointment be able continually with deep joy to experience that men and women live from his wretched service in a hidden depth; that the world lives from this; and that in the middle of what is often a discouraging sowing God's harvest is nevertheless growing.

Recognizing God's presence

Thus with its image of the sower the gospel is at the same time an image of the priest, to whom it tells of the misery and the splendour of his ministry. And it is thus also the right guide to the path that our friend is starting on at this moment. It is at the same time a word of encouragement for all of us who are going through this age when the faith is contested. It teaches us to recognize God's closeness and to be full of joy in the assurance that nevertheless, even through our miserable belief and prayer, God's harvest is growing in the world and that what is hidden is stronger than what is big and noisy. And it is also indeed a word of warning that should make us reflect.

For we cannot escape from this gospel so easily that we simply organize things quite neatly along the lines that we are those who are on God's side and 'the others' are those

17

who do not let his word make any progress. Who are these 'others'? We shall have to ask ourselves quite honestly whether to a considerable extent we ourselves do not also belong among them. We shall have to consider whether we ourselves are perhaps not among those of whom Jesus says that they are without depth, that they are like the stony ground that does not let any roots grow. Or, we must go on to ask ourselves, do we perhaps belong to those whom Jesus calls weathervanes, who cannot stand firm but simply let themselves be driven by the current of the age, who are at the mercy of 'them', of the great mass of people; who are continually asking only what 'they' are doing, what 'they' are saying and thinking, and who have never known the sublimity of the truth for whose sake it is worthwhile to stand out against 'them'?

Or do we not all too often belong to those in which the word is suffocated by the undergrowth of the cares of the world and the delight in riches? Or are we counted among those of whom Jesus says that the word does not really penetrate them at all because the devil takes it away; among those therefore who cannot any longer receive anything at all on God's wavelength because the noise of the world has become too loud for them to be able still to pick out the sound of the eternal that speaks in silence; who in the noise of the age no longer have an ear for God's eternity? And must we not in this way think seriously of the danger that at the end we may be counted among those of whom Jesus says that they have lived 'fruitlessly' – in vain? The fruit, however – so the Lord tells us – grows in patience, in the steadfastness of the person who remains standing however the winds of the age may blow.

To be God's seed-corn

So far we have passed over one verse of the gospel, a very hard saying that comes in the middle between the parable and its interpretation. In this Jesus says to the disciples: 'To you it has been given to know the secrets of the kingdom of God; but for others they are in parables, so that seeing they may not see, and hearing they may not understand.' A very gloomy saying. It makes it look indeed as if the sower of the word is in reality only sent out so as to achieve nothing, so as to fail. In the background is the fate of the great prophets of the Old Testament, those witnesses of God whose fate was in the event failure, the fact that the objection they raised against the power of the mighty of this world came to nothing and was in vain – a Jeremiah, an Isaiah, from whose book (6:9) this saying is taken. If one wants to understand it, then one must look beyond Luke's gospel to that of St John, where we find the saying: 'Unless a grain of wheat falls into the earth and dies, it remains alone; but if it dies, it bears much fruit' (Jn 12:24). And in the first chapter Christ is described as the word who was in the beginning, who came into the world but the world received him not, 'but to all who received him... he gave power to become children of God' (Jn 1:12).

Christ himself is God's seed-corn that God has planted in the soil of this world. Christ himself is the word of eternal love that God is sowing upon earth. He is the grain of wheat that must die in order to ripen and bear fruit. When in a few moments we celebrate the eucharist together we shall hold God's grain of wheat in our hands: the bread that is Christ, the Lord, himself; the fruit that has grown a hundredfold from the death of the grain of wheat and has become the bread of the entire world. Thus the bread of the eucharist is for us at once the sign of the cross and the sign of God's great and joyful harvest. It looks back to the cross, to the grain of wheat that died. But it also looks forward in anticipation to God's great wedding feast to which many will come from east and west, from north and south (cf. Mt 8:11); indeed, this wedding feast has already begun here in the celebration of the holy eucharist, where men and women of all races and classes can be God's happy guests at table.

It is the priest's finest and sublimest ministry that he can be the servant of this holy meal, that he may transform and distribute this bread of unity. For him too this bread will have a double meaning. It will to start with remind him too of the cross. At the end he too must somehow be God's grain of wheat: he cannot be content with giving only words and external actions, he must add a piece of his heart's blood – himself. His fate is tied to God. What that means we have heard in the epistle. It means many kinds of external contestation and failure, the consciousness of not having really been the grain of wheat, and perhaps this is indeed the most oppressive and difficult of the lot, the realization of how pathetic what one has done is measured against the immensity of one's task. Those who know this will understand why the priest says before the Preface every day: 'Pray, brethren, that my sacrifice and yours may be acceptable to God, the almighty Father.' And he will let many kinds of thoughtless talk

21

pass and instead hearken to the complete urgency of this summons to share in bearing this sacred divine burden.

But even for the priest the grain of wheat does not simply point to the cross. For him too it is a sign of God's joy. To be able to be the grain of wheat, the servant of the divine grain of wheat Jesus Christ, can at the same time make man glad in the depths of his heart. In the midst of weakness the triumph of grace is fulfilled, as once again we have heard in the epistle from Paul, who experienced the immense joy of God precisely in his wretchedness. Not without embarrassment does the priest learn how through his weak and petty words people can smile in the last moment of their life; how through what he says people find meaning again in the ocean of meaninglessness, meaning on the basis of which they are able to live; and he learns with gratitude how through his ministry people discover the glory of God. He learns how through him God does great things, through his very weakness, and is full of joy that God has found someone as mean as him worthy of such mercy. And in learning this he becomes at the same time aware that God's joyful wedding feast, his harvest of a hundredfold, is not just a promise in the future but has already begun among us in this bread that he is empowered to distribute, to transform. And he knows that to be able to be a priest is at once the greatest demand and the greatest gift.

So we can well understand that today the Church allows the priest to pray after holy communion once again what he is able to say every day in the Office with the psalmist of the Old Covenant: 'And I will come to the altar of God, the God of my joy' (Ps 43[42]:4). We want to ask God that he will always let something of the splendour of this joy, if it is necessary, fall on our life; that he may give the radiance of this joy ever more deeply and purely to this priest who today for the first time comes before the altar of God; that he will still continually shine upon him when he does so for the last time, when he comes before the altar of eternity in which God shall be the joy of our eternal life, our never-ending youth. Amen.

II

SURRENDERING TO HIS WILL

'Follow me' (Lk 9:51-62)

The gospel of unconditional discipleship shows us who Jesus is in the reflection of the figure of the prophet Elijah. 'Here is greater than Elijah.' What this saying means is here developed and made visible step by step. Jesus appears as one who is travelling, , having 'set his face to go to Jerusalem', going towards the days 'for him to be received up'. Because he is the one who will be 'received up' into the glory of God, but must at the same time remain visibly present in this world, he must call people to follow him as his disciples.

Following Jesus in discipleship is not meant here in the general sense in which it applies to all men and women, in other words discovering how to accompany the Lord on his journey: it is meant in the particular sense prefigured by the Old Testament with Moses and Elijah, in the sense of following in an office or ministry, in a particular task, being included in a particular mission. What is

25

meant is therefore what will later be called the 'apostolic succession', the priesthood of the Church. So this gospel, precisely because it is entirely a gospel of the mystery of Jesus Christ, is at the same time a gospel of the ministry of the priesthood. It speaks to us at this moment when we are aware of the great historical crowd of those who have heard and accepted this summons, when we are touched by the question of the future and the summons of the present.

But let us simply listen to this gospel and follow it step by step as against the background of the figure of Elijah it lets Jesus become visible to us and challenges us.

'Being received up'

The first thing is that Jesus is going to be 'received up', as Luke mysteriously puts it on the basis of Elijah. For what is exceptional about the figure of Elijah and lifts him up above all the other men of God of the Old Covenant and places him alongside Moses, if not from one point of view above him, is that he did not, like all other men and women, descend into the underworld, into the night of death, but that he was taken up and remained someone living in the kingdom of the living. He was someone who had been preserved for the last hour and was therefore looked forward to for the end of the world.

He was someone who was taken up, and his taking up took place in a fiery chariot by means of which the radiant and burning power of the heavenly world seemed to reach into ours so as to bear him there. 'Here is greater than Elijah.' If Jesus wanted to be greater than Elijah, then he too must be taken up, and taken up in a way greater and more exciting than that fiery journey that Elisha was able to gaze after.

And in the event the gospel shows Jesus as someone taken up. But the fiery chariot in which he travels and after which now not only Elijah but the whole of history is gazing (we heard in the reading: 'They will look upon him whom they pierced') – this fiery chariot is of course something quite different from what people would have liked to imagine, awaiting something dramatic, a powerful sign from God. The stations of this fiery chariot are Gethsemane, Caiaphas, Pilate, the way of the cross, Golgotha. The vehicle in which he ascends and as it were flings open the door of heaven is the cross, or more correctly the power of his creative love which reaches into death itself and thereby bridges the boundary between heaven and earth. His fiery chariot is the love of the cross, and this is a vehicle which does not only carry Elijah but is now constructed for us all. He wants as it were to invite all of us on to this vehicle: there we can be taken up with him into the promise of life and the overcoming of death.

If one compares Elijah and him 'who is greater' then that strange occurrence that Elijah was made to experience at Horeb and that remained incomprehensible even to himself becomes understandable, the lesson that God is to be found not in the fire and not in the storm but in the still small voice, in the gentle and hardly perceptible sign of good-ness and love. This is what is greater than the storm of Elijah, the new vehicle that carries not just him but all of us. We have all been shown how the closed door of life opens: how people can move upwards, towards him of whom it is said: 'In my house are many mansions.'

Fire that renews

Another occurrence follows: Jesus sends the two sons of thunder, James and John, out in advance to find accommodation in Samaria, on the way towards Jerusalem. But since the Samaritans reject Jerusalem they naturally will not put up pilgrims to that city. Once again, as at the beginning, he finds that 'there was no room for them in the inn'. On this earth he has nowhere to lay his head; he is the one who everywhere is not wanted.

Now it is reported of Elijah that three times he called down fire from heaven on those who opposed him and wanted to arrest him and that it burnt them up. It counted as one of his great demonstrations of power that fire from heaven was at his command as the force of judgement. So the two sons of Zebedee expected – and one could really say they were quite right to do so – that he who is greater than Elijah would now call down fire on Samaria and let the inhospitable town and its people suffer judgement. But once again Jesus's response is something different. To be able to understand it we must read the gospel here together with Acts, in the eighth chapter of which Luke tells us Jesus's final and definitive response.

After the execution of Stephen the young Christian community had to flee from Judaea. It began to become a universal Church by having to move into what was previously unknown and impassable territory. So messengers arrive, the deacon Philip comes to Samaria, proclaims the word of Jesus, and those who had not accepted the earthly Jesus now say 'yes' to him: they open themselves to the message of the faith. Full of joy, Philip can spread the news in Jerusalem: Samaria has accepted the faith. Now John will go back there, this time with Peter: they lay hands on those who had come to believe and impart the Holy Spirit to them. They let Pentecost come about there – and this is the fire that is Jesus's response: the fire of Pentecost, the fire of his transforming word in which the power of his mercy and his renewal is present and opens people who have been opposed to each other so that because of it they help each other. His new fire is not destructive.

The fire that he wanted to kindle in the world is the power of the Holy Spirit. This is the fire that comes from his fiery chariot of the cross, opens people and gives them new hope, a new way, new life. And again, how gentle his fire clearly is as opposed to the annihilating power of Elijah, and how much greater it is. For it is little power to be able to annihilate. That is very easily done. Real power is to be able to build up, to give life, to open hearts, to transform. This is Jesus's fire, his judgement of new life.

Leaving one's own

Finally comes the third element, following Jesus in discipleship. There are three men whom Jesus encounters here, and in them as in his answers to them is mirrored what discipleship means, what priesthood means. To begin with it is striking that Jesus gives a chilly response to those who are pressing after him and themselves want to follow him. What this is trying to say is that discipleship, or let us just call it by its proper name of priesthood, is not something one can pick out for oneself. It is not something one can devise as a way of being able to attain security, earn one's bread, reach a social position. One cannot simply choose it as a means whereby one finds certainty, friendship, security; how one might construct one's life for oneself. It can never simply be one's own provision, one's own choice. Priesthood, if it is right, is not something one can give oneself nor seek oneself. It can only be a response to his will and to his summons.

What is always needed is that we should come out of what is simply our own will, simply the idea of being able to bring ourselves to realization and of what we could make of ourselves and wanted to have, in order to let ourselves be led by him, indeed let ourselves be led where we do not want to go. If this basic will is not present to enter into another will and become one with this, to let oneself be led where we had not reckoned on going, then the priestly way is not being trod and could only become a disaster. Priesthood rests on having this courage to say 'Yes' to another will, to respond to the summons of the other, so as thereby ever more step by step to gain the great certainty that, surrendered to this will, we are not annihilated, not destroyed, but even in all the directions that cut across us enter for the first time into the truth of our own being. We are in this way closer to ourselves than if we simply clung to ourselves. To follow him, to give this assent – 'I am here, I am ready' – is therefore always an Easter event. It has to do with following the cross, with leaving what is one's own, with letting doing just what one likes and caring just for oneself be frustrated, with our becoming free by means of leaping into the unknown of this other will that is at the same time what is ultimately known. From the cross and the resurrection of Jesus Christ we know it as the will and the power which in truth sustains the world and all of us.

The second man the Lord encounters raises objections that are undoubtedly reasonable. He would like to wait until his father dies and conduct his own affairs for as long as is necessary for everything to be concluded in peace, brought to an end and handed over in good order to someone else. After this he wants to come to Jesus. But who knows when that will be? Will he still then be able to rise up and follow Jesus? What is made clear to us here is that assent to Jesus' summons has priority and demands totality. That means it takes precedence and demands the totality of our being. One cannot simply offer a piece of oneself, a portion of one's time and one's will. In that case one has not answered this summons that is so great that it really demands and fills a whole life, but only fills it if it is offered totally.

This also means that there is a moment of Jesus Christ which one cannot put off and calculate and say: 'Yes, I want to all right, but at the moment it is still too risky for me. At the moment I still want to do this and that.' One can miss the moment of one's life, and with prudence gamble away the real worth of one's life never again to be able to recover it. There is the time of being called in which the decision is present, and it is more important than what we have thought out for ourselves and what is in itself quite reasonable. The reason of Jesus and his summons have precedence: they come first. This courage to defer what seems so reasonable to us in favour of the greater thing that he is, is decisive not only in the first moment but continually on all parts of the way. It is only in this way that we really come close to him.

Having the courage to be near the fire

The third man in this little drama likewise wants to settle things that are waiting at home to be settled. He too has not yet quite got time, but he too is told: 'I have need of all of you'. There is no such thing as half-time or half-hearted priesthood. It is something that needs the person who gives himself and not a part of his time or ability.

Thus we are led back once again to Elijah, to the great scene in which all this is really summed up. Elisha would like to be his successor. And Elijah says to him: 'That is difficult. You can only if you are able to stand by when I am taken up; if you can be near the fire.' It then turns out like this. This saying of Elijah translates into practical terms what we have heard from Jesus's words about following him: discipleship demands that we have the courage to stand by his fiery chariot; that we have the courage to be near the fire which he came to cast upon the earth that it might be kindled. Origen quotes a saying of Jesus that had been handed down: 'Who is near me is near the fire.' Someone who does not want to get burnt will shrink back from him. Belonging to assent to discipleship is the courage to let oneself be burnt by the fire of the Holy Spirit. It is only if we have the courage to be near this fire, if we let ourselves become those who burn, that we can kindle his fire on this earth, the fire of life, of hope and of love.

This fundamentally is ever and again the core of the summons: that we must be ready to be burnt by him, to let ourselves be set on fire, with our hearts burning with the power of his word. If we are half-hearted and slow we cannot kindle any fire in this world, we cannot provide any power of transformation.

Proclaiming joy

But then there is still a saying where Jesus tells us: 'Leave the dead to bury their own dead; but as for you, go and proclaim the gospel, go and proclaim the joyful message.' Work in this world in order to have and possess things is fundamentally concern for what is dead. 'But as for you, leave the dead work of this world and proclaim joy' – that is the real core of the summons that the Lord directs to those who are to carry his word further. To proclaim joy – for this reason Paul called the servants of the gospel 'ministers of your joy'. However much we may talk of the passion of Jesus it is precisely from the midst of this that real joy emerges. The fact that our life in this world is not a life directed towards death, a life that begins and ends in nothing, but a life that from the start is willed by an infinite love and moves towards it – this is shown in the fiery chariot of Jesus Christ. We find this joy of his if we have the courage to let ourselves burn with the message of the Lord. And if we have found it then we can set others on fire, because we are then servants of joy in the midst of a world of death.

We want to ask the Lord that he will let us enter into this light, the fire of his joy. We want to thank him for the fact that over all these four hundred years people have continually put their hand to the plough here without looking back. We want to ask him that at this time too he will find many who will give him their entire assent. We want to ask him that he will give us the courage to put our hand to the plough in order to become ministers of his joy in this world. Amen.

III

HAVING COMPLETE CONFIDENCE
IN HIM

'And many shall rejoice...' (Lk 1:5-17)

Prayer that is heard and granted

Your prayer is heard, the archangel Gabriel said to Zechariah when he told him that his wife was to bear him a son, John the Baptist. This phrase, I think, can provoke us to reflection in a multitude of ways. The birth of this son, who at the same time ushers in the turning-point of the age, the redemption of the world, is hearkening to the prayer of a human being. It takes place as the response to the cry that a human being had made to the Lord. Prayer does not go into a vacuum; nor is it merely something like a kind of psychotherapy which we use to gather our spiritual forces together and try to bring them once more into balance; nor is it a kind of pious fiction to exercise and calm our souls. Prayer is directed at reality. It is heard and hearkened to. God therefore is someone who has the power, the ability, the will and the patience to listen to people. He is so great that he can be present even for those who are small. And though the world is bound by firm ordinances it is not such as to be withdrawn from the power of love that is God's power. God can answer.

We can perhaps go even one step further and say that whatever God does is always a response to this kind of appeal in prayer by men and women; not because God has the style of some great potentate who likes to be asked before he grants something. No; it is because of the fundamental nature of things that it must be so, because it is only when man becomes someone who prays, when he transcends himself, when he surrenders himself, when he perceives and accepts God as reality and opens himself to him and for him, it is only then that the door of the world opens for God and the space is created in which he can act for us men and women and on us. God is indeed always with us, but we are not always with him, says St Augustine. It is only if we accept his presence, by opening our being to him in prayer, that God's activity can really become action on us and for us men and women.

There is yet another thing that seems worth reflecting on in this phrase. It is the question: what was Zechariah actually praying for? He was old and his wife was barren. When the angel promised him a son he rejected this as something absurd that he did not expect from God, as something that as it were he did not include among the things it made sense to pray for. From that we can see clearly that for a long time he had no longer prayed for a son but rather for more than this, for something greater, for what the Bible calls the consolation of Israel, the redemption of the world.

Quite obviously Zechariah belonged to those of whom Luke says when describing the righteous Simeon that they were 'looking for the consolation of Israel' (Lk 2:25). He says the same of the two disciples on the road to Emmaus. When Zechariah was young he too would certainly have prayed for a son. Then the time came when he began to become unimportant and irrelevant to himself and no longer asked for himself; but nor did he lapse into bitterness and fatalism as if the world no longer concerned him and God, who had not hearkened to him, could be indifferent to him. His life had become freer, greater and richer. He had trusted in God not

41

less but more, and prayed to him for the divine gift of the salvation of Israel and included in this, as it must be on the basis of scripture, the salvation of the world.

I think we ourselves can learn to pray from this: not only in the sense of letting ourselves be given fresh courage to pray but also in the sense of receiving an education in prayer. Certainly, God is good, he is there also for the things and the people that are small. For that reason we are able without embarrassment to bring before him all those quite personal small things that are so large and important for us. But at the same time prayer must become a way for ourselves on which gradually we learn to see more. It must not end in us shutting ourselves off in our egoism. Through prayer we must become freer, take ourselves less and him more seriously, and thus find our way to the real point of prayer: to ask God for the salvation of the world – even today. Even today we must have confidence in him that he, and he alone, is in the position to give the world salvation at this moment. When we as Christians move away from this conviction and are of the opinion that this is something we have to do ourselves, when we no longer confide anything to God but at the most let him into our private world, then the door is shut against him and the world becomes uncontrollable and beyond salvation. To confide everything to him, to learn to pray and to dare to pray for the whole of a lifetime: that is where these words from the Bible want to lead us.

We could therefore say that this Zechariah can be summed up in the single phrase that he is a person who prays. And that means that he is a person who believes. And that again means that he is a person who hopes. To put it another way, he does not simply believe that somewhere perhaps there is a higher being of which otherwise he does not know anything and which does not draw attention to itself. Rather he believes that God is God; and that means that neither is the world a matter of indifference to him nor has it fallen out of his control. It means that we must only open the world to him, because he wants to act and can act even if he does something other than what we had conceived in our prayers. He acted differently from what the young Zechariah had expected and differently yet again from what the older Zechariah had expected: so very differently that Zechariah had to begin by being struck dumb in order to learn God's language once again.

If this kind of reflection helps us to see a little what kind of a person this was, then the fact that he was a priest becomes completely important, as well as the fact that his wife too was a daughter of Aaron and that as a consequence John the Baptist was a priest. Priest and prophet do not get in each other's way but in keeping with God's will the last prophet of the Old Covenant, the great prophet of the New Covenant was a priest. This shows the unity of God's activity, demonstrated in actual fact as a unity of priesthood and prophecy. In keeping with this priesthood is not first of all a bundle of activities but is a challenge to our being, a way of life. It is made clear in Zechariah: he is a man who is in conversation with God, a man for whom God is reality, a man who believes him and who trusts him and who through all the transformations of his life does not cease to struggle with God and who clings to him in all the defeats he encounters. 'I shall not leave you and you will bless me.'

If today priesthood and prophethood are often presented to us as opposites – priesthood as what is ossified and institutional, prophethood as what is free, creative and renewing; if in addition worship and social action are contrasted – worship once again as mere pomp in which man establishes himself and clings to himself and social action as liberation and renewal; then here we see that this is not how it is. Only prophecy that springs from being moved by God, from God coming first, can really be from God. The reverse applies that priesthood too is only right when it is from the power of prayer that it comes to proclaim the word and thus to change the world, because prayer extends farther than all our activities: it constantly embraces the whole world which we can then share in embracing if we regard it and affect it on the foundation of God.

For this reason contrasts of this kind are misleading and mean that we do not grasp either priesthood or prophethood correctly any longer. Certainly, there is a degenerate form of priesthood, a danger – in the Old as well as in the New Testament – just as there are degenerate forms of prophecy. In the Old Testament false prophecy is condemned by the prophets no less harshly than the priesthood. Priesthood falls into decay when it is seen only as an opportunity to earn one's living, when it is only a job by which we have a position in the world and struggle along to maintain our social standing, when God becomes a means for us. Then it has become a complete caricature of itself and thus has turned into the opposite of the new departure of the New Covenant and the message of Jesus Christ. But this temptation exists in all ages. Priesthood and prophecy are not opposed to each other; rather, false priesthood and false prophecy are opposed to their true forms. Seen in this way this gospel becomes much more urgent and vivid than if it allowed us merely to reject one of two orders and we could then praise ourselves for being on the right side.

In this way the text becomes a question directed to our consciences, how things stand with ourselves. In the old ritual for the ordination of the priest there was the disturbing phrase: Sat periculosum est hoc, what you are starting on is extremely dangerous. Have we really accepted this knowledge into our lives? Is it really clear to us that having to do with God directly every day and to have this as our vocation can be dangerous, because that can mean that God's presence becomes something normal for us? Being alarmed at this must continually challenge us afresh to take on ourselves the humility of believing, the risk of serving. We must be people who pray, believe and hope.

What we should do

If the priest's being thus comes before his doing, the angel's words also reveal the answer to the question of what we priests should do. What John does now stands before us as eminently priestly activity, as a combination of the priesthood and prophecy of the Old Covenant. And both ultimately belong together in the priesthood of the New Testament. The essential nature of this New Testament priesthood is revealed in this connection. What should therefore be done now is summed up in the phrase 'to make ready for the Lord a people prepared' (Lk 1:17).

I think we can all, each in his own way, reflect on how this should come about. The text itself gives us various indications, from which I would like to select only one or two.

The first thing is that it is said there that he is to lead people to God. In practice it is always a question of us arousing faith, of us leading people out of lethargy and despair and through our faith giving them the courage to see God as reality in this world and in life. It is only when this is the case that the world can live and exist.

Then a second thing is said that is rather difficult to translate. Our German common translation puts it by saying he will lead the disobedient to justice. The Greek says ἀπειθεῖς ἐν φρονήσει δικαίων. One can translate it as: 'He will lead the unbelievers to the way of thinking of the just' or 'to the wisdom of the just.' One can finally also translate it as: 'He will bring those in rebellion to the reason of justice.' All this is interconnected. Thus something very important becomes visible here: that faith is not some backwoods idea that we attach to our real expèriences and bring along with us as our spiritual luggage; and that rebellion, doing it oneself ('building a better world'), is not the last cry of reason but that on the contrary the person who rebels and insists on doing it all himself or herself is the person who does not understand and does not perceive who he or she is and what the world is. Faith is not some abstruse philosophy but finding one's way to wisdom, to understanding, to objectivity, to becoming aware of the whole of reality.

I think we should find this courage once again: to recognize faith as the real objectivity, as the understanding that accepts the world in its true language. Our whole being tells us that we could neither have made ourselves nor can make ourselves, that we are dependent on each other and ultimately are all dependent on what is not within our power. If we are alert we can perceive, through all the obfuscations of the world and our own achievements, that this mysterious other that has shown its face in Jesus Christ is not some dangerous demon but the living God who loves us and intercedes for us. Faith is being led to real objectivity. We are only moral and believing if we do not just let ourselves be swept along by some great idea but if we ask after the correct objectivity and have the courage to hold fast to its sobriety.

This was one of the great tasks of the Baptist in his age: in the face of the charismatic liberation movements which were present and which finally succeeded in destroying Israel completely and wiping it off the face of the map for nearly two thousand years, to proclaim the courage of sober rationality and objectivity, to give people the strength by looking to God to endure the patience of reason.

Establishing peace

Let us now turn to another very odd saying of this gospel: John is called 'to turn the hearts of the fathers to the children' (Lk 1:17). That means he is engaged on a mission of peace. Every priest is in fact entrusted with a mission of peace; for it is only where peace exists that there can be a space for God. John is called to establish or at least to work towards establishing peace within families, peace between the generations, and on this basis peace with God.

But how does peace come about? Not through demonstrations and slogans, certainly not through violence and through a moralistic approach that is detached from objectivity and thereby destroys the foundations of morality. A nation can destroy itself from within without the help of any external war by losing the capacity for reconciliation, for peace; if in fact it can no longer believe in the power of good and knows only the language of force, which is the language of destruction. The priest is there to be the messenger of peace by giving people the courage to become reconciled. This is something he can only give them if he opens their heart to be moved by God's own infinite forgiveness.

I am always profoundly moved by the fact that the last petition but one in the Our Father – forgive us our trespasses as we forgive those who have trespassed against us – is the only one which the Lord provided with a commentary that is also a demand: 'as we forgive those who have trespassed against us'. If you do not forgive each other – that is what is included here – how should the

Father forgive you? But in our text it is above all the other side that is addressed here, the genuinely human aspect of this matter. The basic cell of all human society is the family. It is only in the family and on the basis of the family that the togetherness of love can overcome the opposition of otherness to true community. In it the generations must learn to understand each other. On the recovery of the family depends a nation's capacity for peace. If the family no longer brings man and woman, old and young into relation with each other, people's fundamental relationships turn into a free-for-all battle. For this reason the turning of the fathers to the children is the pre-condition for the beginning of the Messianic peace. And the destruction of families is therefore the surest indication of the Antichrist, the destroyer of peace disguised as the bringer of liberation and peace.

Among experts the question is asked: yes, but who really has to turn over a new leaf? Must the fathers turn to the young people or the young people to their fathers? There can of course be a great deal of discussion on this. But I think that if we read the text of the gospel correctly along with its Old Testament prehistory then it becomes clear that it is not the ones who have to turn to the others but that both must turn over a new leaf by both having afresh the courage to believe in God. It is only in this way that they will learn to understand and accept each other. It is only by the turning of the heart to God that there can arise the courage of togetherness, trust in people and thus the capacity to love them and to sustain and endure their otherness.

Filled with rejoicing and joy

Finally I would like briefly to refer to another phrase in this gospel, once again taken from the angel's message: 'You will have joy and gladness, and many will rejoice' (Lk 1:14). When Jesus approaches joy springs up. Luke, the evangelist who composed his gospel and the Acts of the Apostles so carefully, has not lost sight of this thread. The last sentence of his gospel tells us that when the disciples had seen the Lord ascend they went away, their hearts filled with joy (Lk 24:52).

Acts takes this up again: they broke bread together and did so full of rejoicing and joy (Acts 2:46). They went away when they had seen the Lord ascend – their hearts full of joy. From a purely human point of view what we would expect is 'full of confusion'. But no: anyone who has seen the Lord not just from the outside, who has let his or her heart be moved by him, who has accepted the crucified one and, precisely because he or she has accepted the crucified one, knows the grace of the resurrection, such a person must be full of joy. In the acceptance of the cross the resurrection becomes visible and the world is renewed, the heart full of joy. When we hear this we note how far away we still are from the Lord, from the moment with which Luke concludes his gospel.

We wish to ask the Lord that he will move us and give us his presence and that of us too it will become true that 'you will have joy and gladness, and many will rejoice'. Amen.

IV

WITHOUT HIM EVERYTHING IS IN VAIN

'I am going fishing' (Jn 21:1-14)

Rarely in a biblical passage can one detect the Easter joy of Jesus's disciples so directly as in the gospel of Christ's appearance by the lake of Tiberias. The freshness of the morning by the sea of Galilee gives us some inkling of the morning joy of the emerging Church in which everything is a matter of departure, beginning, hope. The lake, with the broad expanse of its waters merging at the horizon with the blue of the sky, becomes an image for the Church's open future in which in the distance heaven and earth come into contact: it is with confidence and full of hope that one can dare to set sail on the sea of the time that is to come, because Jesus is standing on the bank and because his word accompanies the journey.

On his word

Into the images of recollection that he spreads before us the evangelist has at the same time interwoven an entire image of the Church that is both a promise and a pointer. This image has very many different layers: I would like to try to illuminate merely two characteristics from it. First is the encounter with Jesus after the long night of wasted effort. He stands on the bank; he has passed through the waters of time and death, and now he stands on the bank of eternity, but it is precisely from there that he sees his own and is with them. He asks the disciples for something to eat.

This is part of the mystery of the risen Jesus, of the humility of God: he asks men and women for their contribution. He needs their assent. The Lord asks us to set out for him. He asks us to become fishers for him. He asks us to trust him and to act according to the guidance of his word. He expects us to take this word of his as more important than our own experiences and perceptions. He asks us to act and to live on the basis of his word.

But then something remarkable happens. When the disciples return Jesus does not need their fish. He has already prepared breakfast, and now invites the disciples to eat it; he is the host who provides them with food. The gift is mysterious but nevertheless not hard to decipher. The bread is he himself:

'I am the bread of life.' He is the grain of wheat that dies and now bears fruit a hundredfold and is abundant for everyone until the end of time. His cross on which he gave himself is the miraculous multiplication of loaves, the divine overcoming of the attempt by the devil to catch people with bread and dramatics. Only love can bring about the true multiplication of bread. Material gifts, what is quantitative, always diminish through being divided.

Love however increases the more it gives itself. Jesus is the bread, and he is also the fish that for our sake has gone down into the water of death to look for us there and to find us. This is the lesson of the breakfast to which Jesus invites his own on the borderline of time and eternity, the eucharist. 'Come and eat,' he says to us and thus enables us already to cross the boundary of time and death.

To give everything in order to receive everything

This makes clear a first image of the Church: the Church is first of all a eucharistic community. It is there that there takes place the new thing that distinguishes the Church from all other communities. God affects us. God gives himself to us. God becomes our bread so that we begin to live from him and thus truly to live. Time and eternity interpenetrate each other: that which is stronger than death enters into our time. We receive a food that does not dissolve in dying away and coming into being; we receive a food that lasts and leads us into that which is lasting. And in this way we become a community: the community based on the eucharist, on the Easter mystery of the grain of wheat that died.

But what does that mean? How does it work out? If we want to answer these practical questions correctly then what seems to me quite important is the paradox we have just noticed. First of all Jesus asks the disciples for something to eat: they must set out, act according to his word, to meet this request. But on their return it comes out that he is the giver. This apparent contradiction is not a lack of logic on the part of the narrator or indeed of the Lord. Rather it reveals the inner dimensions of the eucharist and the inner dimensions of the Christian life in general. It is not a question of some kind of trickery: first you must give and then you get something in return. It is rather a question of an indispensable internal cohesion that once again has a number of different aspects. I can only indicate briefly a few of them.

When Jesus asks the disciples if they have any fish they do not yet recognize him. They must give to the unknown person who is hungry. It is only when they themselves learn this giving that there ripens in them the love that makes them capable of accepting the new food, the quite different bread, that God himself becomes for us in Christ. The social dimension is not something stuck on to the eucharist from the outside; it is rather the context without which the eucharist cannot take shape at all.

The same thing happened with the multiplication of the loaves. The boy must first of all surrender the precious gifts of his mother; then every individual had to share out what seemed to be only just enough for himself or herself. That was how the multiplication of the loaves happened, and that is how it always happens. And in this something yet more profound is accomplished: the disciples who set out to catch fish for Jesus must fundamentally give themselves. It is only someone who gives himself or herself who discovers that everything has already been given to him or her, that he or she is always giving only *de tuis donis ac datis* – from what he or she has received. First we must give ourselves in order then to receive God's gift. Ultimately everything comes from God. And yet God's gift cannot reach us if we ourselves have not first become those who give. Ultimately everything is grace, for the great things of the world, life, love, God, one cannot make but only receive as a gift. And yet we can only be given gifts if we ourselves are those who give gifts. It is only to the extent that we give that we receive; only to the extent that we follow that we are free; only to the extent that we sacrifice that we receive what we could not in any way earn.

Thus here in this simple story we find explained a question that since the century of the Reformation has led to passionate tensions within Christendom. Giving everything and receiving everything are not mutually exclusive but mutually inclusive: that is shown here. Thus what holds true primarily and as a fundamental truth is that Christ's sacrifice is once and for all and sufficient for us all. It is true that in this we all can only be the receivers and that it would be a presumption to want to add anything to this. And yet at the same time it is without contradiction true that his sacrifice can only become ours if we ourselves have set out to give Christ everything. The fact that Christ's sacrifice is given to us in the sacrifice of the Church does not diminish Christ's gift but makes the greatness of its humanity visible, since God acts in a human way. It is precisely in his greatest mysteries that he accepts and incorporates human nature in the most profound way.

But now we must return to the gospel. We said that in reflecting anew on the images of recollection the images of what is essential and lasting emerge for John. In the images of the morning in Galilee he lets us recognize the image of the Church, the essential nature of Christian life. A first image of the Church that we found is the pointer to its eucharistic core. The Church is the eucharistic community. It is unity with the Lord. At the same time it was made clear what depths of human and divine reality are comprised in the simple saying of the Risen One: 'Come and eat.'

To receive the eucharist means to pace out all the dimensions of being human. We only receive it if we follow the entire path of Jesus's Easter mystery that he shares with us. But this includes not just a liturgical component and not just a spiritual or religious one but also one that is apparently quite secular: our readiness to make the effort to ensure that those whom we do not know but who need our help can eat. Because the eucharist includes the entire nature and essence of man and the whole reality of Jesus Christ to such an extent, it is for that reason alone that it can build a Church that is more than a club for one's leisure time – a community that reaches into eternity.

Fullness and unity

Now, however, I would like briefly to draw attention to a second aspect of the image of the Church that seems to me to shine through the story told in this gospel. This is this remarkable story of the hundred and fifty-three fishes. One can certainly take it for granted that John did not include this number in his gospel just for fun. His gospel and even more the Apocalypse continually address us through the symbolism of numbers, and thus the Fathers were certainly right to look for the meaning which the evangelist wished to encode by providing this number. Of course one cannot obtain certainty about the right interpretation of this passage. That would indeed contradict the nature of the symbolic message which aims at arousing the attention to what cannot be pinned down in exact concepts. But one can be reasonably secure in following interpretations which correspond to the internal direction of the gospel as a whole and thus do not introduce anything new but throw fresh light on its general content from a new side. Using this criterion two interpretations above all seem to me to be illuminating.

The first one, supported by the Fathers, points to the fact that seventeen is a factor of a hundred and fifty-three. But seventeen is the number of the peoples mentioned in St Luke's account of Pentecost; it is a number of totality, of fullness. Just as these seventeen peoples in the Pentecost story point to the Church composed of all peoples and nations, so do the hundred and fifty-three fish point to the extent of the Church of Jesus Christ, which is meant to shelter all kinds of fish within itself and give them room. It is an image of the catholicity of the Church, in which there are many mansions: room for all. The Church of the many mansions, the Church of the many fish that threaten to split the net: what an excellent and at the same time demanding image! For this means first of all that God's first idea about the Church is not the local congregation but the catholic Church in its totality and unity.

The universal Church is not a sum of congregations which combine for the sake of greater efficiency or for other reasons; it is primary, and it gives birth to the congregations. That quite clearly is the message of

Luke's account of Pentecost: even before there were local congregations the Catholic Church already existed, the Church of all peoples and nations, St Luke is telling us. The net with the hundred and fifty-three fish is recapitulating the same insight in the symbolic language of St John. Unity is first; it gives birth to diversity, and gives it its meaning.

This is indeed also quite clear if one considers the inner origin of the Church. Christ is not related to the Church like the founder of some society or association to the body he has founded. Indeed, as contemporary exegesis shows us, he did not in fact found it as an association or society. He did not found it through individual actions but through his being as the grain of wheat that has died. But this then means a quite different relationship. Christ is not a founder whose will one recalls from time to time. He is the ever-present origin of the Church in the eucharist. Hence the Church is not primarily tied to him through all kinds of legal ordinances but is borne by him in the community of being. Paul takes this so far as to say that there is only one elect but that we are all this one through community with Christ (Gal 4:15-29).

The same emerges from the external origin of the Church. It is not some new creation of

Jesus. The people of God has been on its way since Abraham and can always only be one: through Jesus its boundary-posts have merely been extended to the ends of the earth and driven in more deeply – as far as the trinitarian love of God. While Luke tells us of a first setting-out to sea when the nets tore at the beginning of Jesus's public life, John tells us that although there were so many the net was not torn (cf. Jn 21:11). The net must not tear. The Church is one and must be the space for all the fish of Jesus Christ; the torn body of the crucified one who yet is not broken is the space of our unity.

Much could be said about this; I shall merely in conclusion add the second interpretation of the number one hundred and fifty-three. It points in the same direction and at the same time anticipates the next story in the gospel. It comes from the Jewish scholar Robert Eisler, who pointed out that one hundred and fifty-three is the sum of the numerical values of Simon (seventy-six) and the Greek word for fish, ἰχθῦς (seventy-seven). This interpretation once again points towards the unity of the Church and its catholicity, but it throws a closer light on the historical type of unity. The Church's real unity is always the one fish Jesus Christ. But he linked himself and the unity of his Church to the man whom he called Peter, the rock. In fact the whole account concludes with the commissioning of Peter, to whom is entrusted the task of tending and feeding the flock of Jesus Christ, a flock which is one and which is tended by him as a whole.

Peter and Christ belong together; Peter's boat has become the ship of Christ. Peter stands surety for Christ. If I want to accept him I must accept the actual definite community of the one Church whose shepherd is Peter. It is precisely in this way that the path of Easter is always accomplished. Only if we accept and assent to Christ to this point of definite actuality do we let ourselves be bound and led by him not according to our own will but according to his. What seems quite legal and definite and what is most profound, the core of revelation, are inseparably connected. God is definite and it is precisely in what is definite that he shows himself as divine.

We want to ask the Lord that he will grant us to be in the shoal of the hundred and fifty-three fish of his unbroken net. We want to ask him to grant us to let ourselves be bound and led by him even against our will. We want to ask him that our eyes may be opened and that like Peter we recognize him and learn to say, full of joy: 'It is the Lord.' Amen.

V

THE MINISTRY OF THE WITNESS

'It is the Lord' (Jn 21:1-14)

The reading from Acts (5:27-32,40-41) and the gospel of the Third Sunday of Easter are a witness for Jesus Christ, a witness for his resurrection. They are not telling us the disciples' imagined ideas, for in that case it would have been presumptuous to pitch this witness as the will of God against the will of men and women. In that case it would also have been quite unnecessary to take imprisonment and beatings on oneself for the sake of this witness. It would equally have made no sense to rejoice in the shame they had suffered in public if there were not hidden in this shame a higher glory, the glory of God and the glory of the truth.

God has answered

Testimony that consists only of words does not carry a lot of weight: it can even be false witness. But when with the witness of suffering life itself becomes testimony then other considerations are involved. The apostles bear witness to Jesus with their life because he himself is living, is life, and because they are completely certain of this. The testimony of life applies to him whom they have seen as someone living.

Thus the real message of this day runs: God has answered. God is really God. God has power over the world, power over our life and power even over our dying. God is God. He has power, and his power is the goodness that bestows life – real life. Because the apostles knew this not just as theory but had it burnt into their souls as a living perception, they were full of joy.

The aim of the Church's liturgy is to lead us to receiving this joy, the joy of the redeemed. We receive it to the extent that we perceive Christ, to the extent that we become certain that he is living, that he is truly risen.

The reading and the gospel are therefore testimonies to Christ. He is the real subject of these texts, just as he is the true subject of our liturgy. But in this way, with reference to Christ, the texts of this day also give us a picture of the witness of Jesus Christ.

What is demanded of a witness? The first basic condition becomes clear in the story of the draught of fishes: the apostles return home.

On the bank an unknown person is standing. The disciple whom Jesus loved recognizes him: 'It is the Lord.' Peter gets up, puts his clothes back on and jumps into the water to hurry to meet him. The first condition is therefore that whoever wants to be a witness of Jesus must have seen him himself, must know him. How does that come about? Love knows him, the gospel tells us. Jesus stands on the bank; at first we do not recognize him, but through the voice of the Church we hear: 'It's him.' It is up to us to make a start, to look for him and to approach him. In listening to scripture, in living with the sacraments, in the encounter with him in personal prayer, in the encounter with those whose life is filled with Jesus, in a variety of experiences in our life and in a variety of ways we encounter him, he seeks us, and thus we learn to know him.

To come closer to him in a variety of ways, to learn to see him: that is the primary task of the study of theology. This study speaks fundamentally of nothing at all if the ideas of science are not related to the reality of our life. The more we recognize him himself, the more all the words of tradition begin to speak to us, the more they become ways to him and from him to men and women.

The witness must therefore first of all be something before he or she does something; he or she must become a friend of Jesus Christ so that he or she is not just handing on knowledge at second hand but is really a witness.

What should the witness do?

But then the question arises: what should the witness do? The gospel gives us three answers which are really all a single answer. Before Peter is entrusted with the office of shepherd Jesus asks him: 'Do you love me?' He must love Jesus. Then he is told: 'Feed my lambs.' He must fulfil the duties of a shepherd. And finally he is told: Before, you went your own way. Now another will determine your way and lead you; it is no longer your will that decides where you go but the will of someone else. He must follow: following in discipleship belongs to the ministry of the disciple, and this ministry is a way.

Feeding

Loving, feeding, following: these three key-words are used by the gospel to describe the essential nature of the apostolic office and thus too the essential nature of the priestly ministry. Because loving is the core of everything else, we can content ourselves with reflecting a little more closely on the two other fundamental actions.

Let us begin with feeding and tending. The word refers back to Israel's nomadic period in which it had been above all a people of herdsmen. In today's gospel we find the same thing but illuminated from a different starting point. Jesus's disciples whom he had collected at the Sea of Galilee had originally been fishermen, and it was thus on this basis that he disclosed to them their future calling. 'Henceforth you will be catching men,' Jesus said to Peter the morning he called him (Lk 5:10).

Of all the interpretations of this saying that I have encountered the one that has most impressed me is that of St Jerome. What he says is more or less as follows. When the fish is drawn out of the water it means for it that it has lost the element essential for its life. It can no longer breathe and perishes. But for us men and women what happens in baptism, in becoming a Christian, is the opposite. Hitherto we have been imprisoned in the salt water of the world. We cannot see the light, God's light. We cannot see the expanse of the world. Our sight is shut in by the darkness of the water and pointed downwards, and our life is sunk in the death-world of the salt water. But when in baptism we are drawn out of it then we begin to see the light and then we begin really to live.

I think it is not at all difficult to recognize today how true that is. Life without God and against God, which at first seemed so enticing and liberating, has created in reality only great sadness and increasing anger. Man rages against society, against the world, against himself and against the others; his life seems to him like botched handiwork, man like a mistake on the part of evolution. He has lost the element that is really essential for his life, and everything tastes like salt to him – of death and bitterness. Man is destined to breathe the infinity of eternal love – if he cannot he is in prison and deprived of light. It is only faith that leads us out into the open, as the psalms say.

What then does 'catching men' mean? It means to lead people out into the open, into the broad expanse of God, into the element essential to their life that is intended for them.

Admittedly anyone who is torn away from his or her habitual surroundings always puts up a fight against it, as Plato so vividly described for us in his myth of the cave. Someone who has become used to the sea thinks first of all that his or her life is being taken away if he or she is brought into the light. He or she has fallen in love with the darkness. So being a fisher of men is no comfortable undertaking – but the most wonderful and, humanly speaking, the finest there can be. Certainly it includes many unsuccessful expeditions. But nevertheless it is a wonderful task to accompany people on the way to the light, to the open air, and to teach them to know God's light and openness. When thirty-five years ago I started out on this I was afraid about how it would go. But very soon I found out and went on finding out how true the Lord's promise is that even in this world he returns one's investment a hundredfold – with difficulties, admittedly, but he keeps his word (cf. Mk 10:29-30).

Of course there is still one thing we need to consider: the real core of the art of catching men. In today's gospel Jesus gives the disciples bread and fish to eat. Both symbolize himself. Just as he became the grain of wheat that dies, so he has become the fish. He himself sank into the depths of the sea.

With his whole life he fulfilled the sign of Jonah, letting himself be swallowed up by the belly of the sea. Only someone who gives himself or herself can be a witness, we said earlier. Only someone who like Jesus himself becomes a 'fish' can be a fisher of men.

Discipleship

But with this we have already reached the question of following Jesus in discipleship. Stripped of images what that means is quite simply that the core of feeding and tending the sheep, of the ministry of the shepherd, is following Jesus in discipleship. The shepherd goes ahead, St John's gospel tells us. Only if we ourselves go ahead do we find pasture for the others. And we only go ahead, we only move forward, if we follow him who has gone ahead of all of us, Jesus Christ.

Precisely in connection with the figure of Peter the gospels give us various indications in which it becomes clear what discipleship means. One of the most vivid scenes takes place immediately after Peter's confession that Jesus is the Christ with which the history of the primacy begins. The Lord explained what was special about his kingdom by forecasting his own suffering. And whereas formerly it was more than flesh and blood that spoke through Peter, now flesh and blood speak out quite forcefully when Peter reproaches the Lord for what he said. Jesus's answer is unusually harsh: 'Get behind me, Satan!' (Mk 8:33). Peter had wanted to take the lead, to determine the path Jesus was to follow. Discipleship means no longer finding for oneself the way one is to follow. It means surrendering one's own will to that of Jesus and genuinely letting him take the lead.

Another aspect becomes clear in our story: Peter is on the lake, Jesus on the shore. To reach him Peter quickly hurls himself decisively into the water. Related to this is the uniquely wonderful story of how Peter got out of the boat to go to meet the Lord whom he saw walking on the water. As long as his gaze was fixed on Jesus all was well. The moment he directed his attention to the wind and the waves he began to sink (cf. Mt 14:28-32). He is following a path that defies gravity. He can follow it as long as he lets himself be supported by the new and stronger gravity of the presence of Jesus Christ, in keeping with the saying: 'Be of good cheer, I have overcome the world' (Jn 16:33). Gravity and grace are fighting against each other here.

Following Jesus Christ in discipleship means that we must and can follow a path that is directed against the force of gravity of our natures, against the gravity of egoism, the hankering after what is purely material and after the maximum pleasure that is confused with happiness. Following Jesus in discipleship is a path through the waves whipped up by the storm that we can only follow if we are within the gravitational field of the love of Jesus Christ with our gaze fixed on him, and thus borne up by the new gravity of grace which makes possible for us the path to truth and to God that we would not be able to follow with our own resources. For this reason following Christ in discipleship is more than agreement with a definite programme, more than sympathy and solidarity with a human being whom we regard as a model. We are not just following Jesus, a human being; we are following Christ, the son of the living God. We are following a divine path.

Where does Jesus's path go to? It goes to the resurrection, to the right hand of the Father. It is this entire path that is meant when we talk of following Christ in discipleship. It is only with this that the entire vocation of man is described, that we really reach the goal of undivided and indestructible happiness. And it is only on this basis that one understands why the cross belongs to following Christ (cf. Mk 8:34); one cannot come to the resurrection, to the community of God, by any other way. We must follow this entire path if we want to be the servants and witnesses of Jesus Christ. And every single step is different according to whether one accepts the entire way or is merely carving out for oneself a kind of human party programme. One can only come to Christ if one has the courage to walk on the water and trust oneself to his gravity, the gravity of grace.

Being led where you do not wish to go

Finally right at the end of our story there comes yet another surprising image for following Christ in discipleship: 'You will stretch out your hands, and another will gird you and carry you where you do not wish to go' (Jn 21:18). Probably this is a reference to the death on the cross that Peter will suffer in imitation of Jesus; his hands were stretched out and bound. What was first indicated in the quarrel between Peter and Jesus after the latter's forecast of his passion is here made completely clear: Peter must renounce his own will; no longer does he decide what happens to him. Another girds him.

This story always recalls to my mind a

detail that affected me profoundly at my ordination. At that time after one's hands had been anointed they were bound together, and it was with one's hands bound together that one took the chalice. The chalice – that recalled to my mind Jesus's question to the brothers James and John: 'Are you able to drink the cup that I drink?' (Mk 10:38).

The eucharistic chalice, core of the priestly life, always recalls this saying. And then the hands bound together, anointed with the Messianic ointment of the chrism. The hands are an expression of the power we have to dispose of our own lives; with them we can grab things, take possession of things, defend ourselves. The hands bound together are an expression of powerlessness, of the renunciation of power. They are placed in his hands; they are placed on the chalice. One could say that this shows simply that the eucharist is the core of the priestly life. But the eucharist is more than a rite, than liturgy. It is a form of life. The hands are bound together; I no longer belong to myself. I belong to him and through him to the others. Following Christ in discipleship is a readiness to be bound conclusively – just as he bound himself conclusively to us. The hands bound together are in truth open hands, outstretched hands, as the gospel says. The courage of being bound conclusively, the entire assent – that is discipleship. It is only in this entire assent that we go the whole way we were speaking of before. And only the whole way is the true way, for truth and love cannot be separated. We want to ask the Lord that he will let us understand ever more deeply this mystery of discipleship.

We want to ask him to give us the courage to get out of the boat of our earthly safe-guards and reservations and venture out on the water. We want to ask him that at the right moment he will stretch out his hands to us, take us by the hand and climb into our boat. We want to thank him for having called us to stand before him and serve him. Amen.

VI

IN THE BEGINNING IS LISTENING

'And he called to him those whom he desired'
(Mk 3:13-19)

It is a great joy for me to greet you, this diocese's candidates for the priesthood, and to be able to celebrate the holy eucharist together with you. It is good to see how even today young people make themselves ready to follow the call of Christ: 'I will make you fishers of men.' It is good to know that even today God gladdens the youth, as Psalm 42:4 says in the Vulgate, inspires young people and arouses in them the courage to leave behind the nets of middle-class life, of the family, of the search for a good income, in order to bring this God to others. It is good to experience how in young people the Church itself remains ever young and continually becomes rejuvenated. With their nets they bring a new age, new ideas, new experiences and insights to the country of faith. So the beginning too remains always contemporary. For a seminary indeed means that even today the Lord is going up into the hills and calling those whom he desires. The seminary is these hills of Jesus. The morning in Galilee is not the distant past; here it is fresh and present, the moment in which the day of the Church continually begins anew, no, rather, the day of Jesus Christ dawns until at last the final and definitive morning comes that no longer knows any evening because its sun, the love of the triune God made for ever manifest, does not set.

He went up into the hills

The seminary is the hills into which Jesus goes up in order to call people. In this wonderful brief extract from St Mark's gospel every word is full of meaning. It speaks so directly to us because these are not words which we must laboriously drag back as it were from the far distance into our life. What is there affects us directly: it is our life, our present. Jesus goes up into the hills; he loved the hills as he loved the lake, the flowers of the field and the birds of the air. He loved creation because it was indeed his word that had taken shape, the reflection of the divine mystery out of which he came. So we can say that friendship with Jesus includes joy in creation, in its inexhausted splendour, in the large and small miracles of the universe.

But the fact that the calling of the disciples takes place in the hills means that much more is involved. The hills are the place of Jesus's prayer. They are the place where he is alone, where he turns to the Father. They are an expression for the heights, for the inward ascent above being caught in the affairs of the everyday world. The calling of the disciples comes out of Jesus's conversation with the Father. We can only receive it if we share in making this inward ascent of Jesus. If we want to find and accept our vocation and bring it to maturity we must find Jesus's hills: becoming free of the trammels of everyday life, silence, recollection, turning to the living God. We must arrive at that openness and those heights in which Jesus's voice can be heard.

...and called to him those whom he desired

And that is how it now continues: he called to him those whom he desired. Priesthood only becomes possible if one has learned to hear his voice. It depends on a relationship of dialogue. But it depends above all on his initiative. The form of words used by St Mark's gospel is very emphatic here: he called those whom he desired – not just those who wanted to be called themselves.

There is no right to the priesthood. One cannot choose it as one can choose this job or that. One can only be chosen for it – by him. To be a priest does not belong to the list of human rights, and no one can sue to obtain it. He calls those whom he desires. There are human rights which people are entitled to on account of their God-created nature and for which those who believe in the Creator must unconditionally assume responsibility. But there is also a right of the Lord – to take those whom he wants. For those who have received this call this means: He wants me. There is a will of Jesus concerned with me. I must enter into this will and mature within it. It is the space within which I must live. Our life will become the more fulfilled and free the more we become one with this will in which the profoundest truth of our own self is contained.

He appointed twelve

Let us now take a brief look at the next phrase: 'And he appointed twelve.' This expression emphasizes once again that priesthood is 'made' by Jesus. It is not a product of our own decision, nor can it be brought about by a decision of the community. Nobody on his or her own account can say the words that really belong to him alone: 'This is my body. This is my blood. I forgive you your sins.' No society can empower anyone to do that: only he can. It is precisely this that is the great consolation in all this, that here something that goes beyond all our capabilities enters into history.

It is precisely for this transcending of all our own ability that our heart is continually waiting, that history is continually waiting: for the power to grant forgiveness that alters the past; for the power to summon up a love that is indestructible. Twelve is the number of the tribes of Israel, but it is also the number of the constellations that form the rhythm of the year.

Thus it is made clear that here a new Israel is to be built. But at the same time it is been made clear that this new people stands for harmony between heaven and earth: 'Thy will be done on earth as it is in heaven.' The way that is being opened up here decides on heaven and earth. It brings the two into harmony. And the twelve that are called there become as it were the new constellations of history that point us the way through the centuries.

To be with him

If here suddenly a horizon is opened up that may seem to us almost too splendid and bold, the next words are once again quite down to earth and practical. They answer the question: What are these people being called for? What actually is Jesus's will with regard to them? Two reasons are named: 'to be with him' and 'to be sent out'.

At first glance this seems in fact to be a contradiction. Either, one could say, Jesus wants them to form his entourage and always to accompany him; or he wants people he can send out who then will of course only be with him from time to time. If we transpose this question into the terminology of a later age, then one would say that here the monastic, contemplative vocation and the apostolic vocation seem to be intertwined with each other. We on the other hand distinguish them and are of the opinion that to a considerable extent the one excludes the other.

But it is precisely here that Jesus corrects us. Only someone who is with him can be sent. And only someone who lets himself or herself be sent, who transmits his message and his love, is with him. Of course there are various different kinds and forms of this mission, various different patterns of the aposto-

86

late and of being close to him. I would not want to dispute this here at all. But prior to and transcending all these differences there is a fundamental unity that is indispensable. Apostles are eye-witnesses and, if I may be allowed the term, ear-witnesses. Only someone who knows him, who knows his words and deeds, who has himself or herself experienced him in the encounter of long days and nights – only that kind of person can bring him to others. That is true even today. 'To be with him' – that is the first and fundamental component of the priestly vocation.

Being with him in prayer

If as a bishop or formerly simply as a colleague I have looked into the reasons why a vocation which began with so much enthusiasm and so many hopes has gradually collapsed, what emerged was always the same: at some time silent prayer came to a stop – perhaps because of sheer keenness to get on with everything that had to be done. But now the keenness had become just a shell because its inner impetus had been lost. At some time personal confession had come to a halt and with it a contact with challenge and forgiveness, a renewal from within in the face of the Lord that is indispensable. 'To be with him' – this 'with him' is something one needs not just for a certain initial period so that one could draw on it later. It must always be the core of priestly ministry. But one must practise it and learn it so that in due course it achieves a certain ease and comes to be taken for granted, and thus can be maintained even in difficult times. So I would urge you sincerely to regard this as the fundamental task of your time in the seminary and later of your priestly life: to be with him, to learn to keep your gaze on him, to practise listening to him, to get to know the Lord more and more in prayer and in the patient reading of Holy Scripture.

It is important to cultivate prayer not only when it makes us happy. Just as nothing important in human life can be attained without discipline and method, so too does our inner life need both these. If we listen to a great virtuoso who has a perfect mastery of his or her instrument, we are moved by the ease which simply lets the beauty of the work he or she is playing speak for itself and the relaxed way in which this is apparently taken for granted. But precisely in order for this ease ultimately to exist, in which a masterpiece can be expressed directly and without being masked in any way, a long period of disciplined work is needed beforehand. Our inner life should be no less valuable to us than outward performance, than sport and technical ability. The 'growth of the inner person' is worth our entire commitment and effort; the world needs people who have become inwardly mature and rich; the Lord needs them so that he can call them and send them out.

Preaching and having authority

Finally our text names the two essential elements of apostolic and priestly mission. They are sent out to preach and to have authority to cast out evil spirits. Preaching and authority, word and sacrament are the two fundamental pillars of priestly ministry. They remain so for all time. In the daily life of the priest the two tasks take on a variety of forms. The ministry of the word has many forms, from preaching and instruction to personal conversation. The ministry of the sacrament is not confined only to the moment of liturgical action. It demands the inward preparation of the person administering the sacrament; it demands the guidance of those receiving it. But it is important to take care that we do not let ourselves be pushed away from these fundamental tasks.

After the Council the impression arose here and there that there were more urgent things to do than to proclaim the word of God and to administer the sacraments. Many were of the opinion that one first had to establish a different society before one could again devote time to such things. At the root of such views lay a spiritual blindness that was only able to perceive material values and forgot that men and women *always* need the whole, that both their physical and their spiritual hunger must be answered. Nor can spiritual questions be put off. On the contrary, their postponement or exclusion only incites other problems and makes them even more impossible to solve.

For this reason leading men and women to the living God is never superfluous. It is always the fundamental condition for the best powers of men and women being aroused without which ultimately they cannot live. The more we ourselves are penetrated by the presence of the living God, the more we can bring him to men and women; and the more we too will realize that precisely this kind of genuinely priestly ministry does not pass real life by but has the effect 'that they may have life and have it abundantly' (Jn 10:10).

Finally I would like to direct your attention to a later passage in St Mark's gospel that continues the line begun here (Mk 10:28-31). Jesus's earthly path is coming to its end; the disciples are faced by the question of where all this is really leading. They are concerned about themselves and whether their choice was the right one. Peter says what the others are thinking: 'Lo, we have left everything and followed you.' Matthew makes the meaning of this discreet and yet urgent question clear by adding: 'What then shall we have?' (Mt 19:27). We would expect the Lord to rebuke the timidity, the lack of faith or even the barely disguised selfishness echoed by these words. But this is not the case. The question about where all this is leading is seen by the Lord as entirely justified, and he gives an astonishing answer: 'Truly, I say to you, there is no one who has left house or brothers or sisters or mother or father or children or lands, for my sake and for the gospel, who will not receive a hundredfold now in this time, houses and brothers and sisters and mothers and children and lands, with persecutions, and in the age to come eternal life' (Mk 10:29-30).

What is the astonishing thing about this

answer? The Lord does not just point to the reward in the world to come. He says something very daring and almost unbelievable. This life of yours, he says, will admittedly always remain under the sign of persecutions; it will be a very human life with disputes and distress. But your reward is not simply postponed until the hereafter. You will now already receive a hundredfold. 'Already in this life God gives a hundred for one,' was how Teresa of Avila summed up the content of this saying of Jesus. From everything that is given up for his sake grows a response that multiplies. God is magnanimous and does not let us outdo him in magnanimity. The first thing that belongs to the apostolic ministry is giving things up: celibacy is one of the very precise forms that this kind of giving up must take. Anyone who looks back over his life as a priest after a shorter or longer period knows how true this saying of Jesus is. First one must dare to make the leap. And one cannot try as it were to get back in small change what previously one has paid out in notes: the Holy Spirit does not let itself be deceived, as we know from the story of Ananias and Sapphira. But in the midst of all the disputes that remain it becomes truer from day to day that a large family of brothers and sisters and fathers and mothers and children accrues to him who brings the word of faith to men and women. And continually it becomes true that God gives a hundred for one, even in this world. We must only have the courage to begin by giving one, to dare to make the leap, as Peter dared when, on the morning he was called, he put out to sea on the lake once again against all probability and obtained the sign of what was to come, the miraculous draught of fishes that revealed to him the power of Jesus.

Let us give the miserable one of our abilities, our renunciation of the tiny world of our own; let us ask the Lord day by day for the magnanimity to entrust ourselves to him. Let us go with him. Let us allow ourselves to be sent. So we shall be in good hands. Amen.

'AT YOUR WORD' (Lk 5:1-11)

On priestly spirituality

There has been very much reflection on the priesthood over the last twenty years, and also very much dispute. In all this it has demonstrated more vitality than many rash arguments aimed at leaving it behind as a sacral misunderstanding and replacing it by a purely functional ministry for a limited period. Gradually the presuppositions have become clear that made arguments of this kind seem at first almost irrefutable. The overcoming of prejudices has made once again possible a deeper understanding of the biblical witness in its internal unity of the old and the new covenant, of Bible and Church, so that we are no longer dependent for water on cisterns which in the struggle between different hypotheses first dry up and then offer a miserable trickle, but have access to the living source of the Church's faith through all the ages.

If I perceive rightly, in the future the key-question will be precisely this: how does one in fact read Scripture? At the time when the canon was taking shape, which was in fact also the time when the Church and its catholicity were taking shape, Irenaeus of Lyons was in advance of everyone else in having to face this question, the answering of which is decisive for the possibility or impossibility of ecclesial life. In his time Irenaeus recognized as the principle of a Christianity of adaptation and enlightenment which threatened the Church at that time from its roots up (and which has been labelled *gnosis)* the splitting up of the Bible and the separation of Bible and Church. This fundamental double division was preceded by the internal splitting up of the Church into communities which created their own legitimization by selecting their own sources. The disintegration of the sources of the faith brought about the disintegration of communion and vice versa. Gnosis, which seeks to represent as the real principle the principle of separation, dividing testament from testament, Scripture from Tradition, educated from uneducated Christians, is in truth a phenomenon of disintegration. The unity of the Church, on the other hand, causes to become visible the unity of that from which it lives, and vice versa it is only alive if it draws from the whole – from the many-faceted unity of the Old and New Testaments, of Scripture, Tradition, and the realization in faith of the

Word. But if one has first submitted to the logic of disintegration there is fundamentally nothing more to be put together properly.[1]

Meanwhile it did not strike me as fitting the joyful nature of today's celebration to enter into the scientific quarrel which has been indicated above and which must indeed be fought out before one deals with the details of the biblical witness on such a subject as the priesthood. The joy of this day is itself something like a *locus theologicus*. Fifty years of priesthood are a reality that speaks for itself and gives our reflections an actual context. So I thought it would be right on this occasion not to attempt a scientific lecture on the priesthood but rather something like a spiritual reflection in which without systematic treatment and without claims to scholarship I could meditatively expound a couple of scriptural passages which have become important for me personally.

---

[1] Cf., among the wealth of literature on Irenaeus and *gnosis*, H.J. Jaschke, *Irenäus von Lyon, 'Die ungeschminkte Wahrheit'*, Rome, 1980.

1. Reflections of the priest's images in the accounts of the calling of the disciples in Luke 5:1-11 and John 1:35-42

As my first text I have chosen Luke 5:1-11. This is that wonderful story of the calling of the disciples in which we are told how Peter and his friends after a night of futile labour put out to sea yet again at the word of the Lord. There followed the great draught of fishes so that the nets were nearly torn. Then comes the summons: 'You shall become a fisher of men.' I have a quite particular love for this story because it is bathed in the morning light of first love, a beginning full of hope and readiness. In thinking about it I am always reminded of what was bright and fresh about my own beginning: that joy in the Lord which we used to express in the psalm at the foot of the altar at the beginning of Mass: 'I will go in to the altar of God, to God who giveth joy to my youth' (Ps 42:4 Douai) – to the God in whose presence the joy of being young becomes ever new, because as life itself he is the source of real youth.

But let us come to our text. We are told how people pressed round Jesus because they wanted to hear the word of God. He was standing by the bank of the lake, the fishermen were washing their nets, and Jesus got into one of the two boats that were there, that belonging to Peter. He asked him to put out a little from land, sat down in the boat and taught. Peter's boat became the cathedra of Jesus Christ. Afterwards he said to Simon: 'Put out into the deep and let down your nets.' The fishermen had an unsuccessful night behind them; it seemed pointless to try once again to catch anything now it was morning. But already Jesus has become for Peter so important, so authoritative, that he can say: 'At your word I will do it.' The word of Jesus has become more real than what is apparently empirically certain and real. The Galilaean morning whose freshness one can almost breathe in this picture becomes the image for the new morning of the gospel after the night of futile efforts into which we are always being led by our own exertions and desires. When Peter and his companions return with the laden boats whose cargo they were only able to gather jointly because of the wealth of the gift that had torn their nets, it was not just an outward journey and a piece of manual work that he had behind him. This journey became for him an inward path the course of which Luke indicates to us by framing it with two words. The evangelist tells us that before the draught of fishes Peter addressed the Lord as ἐπιστάτα, which means something like teacher, professor, rabbi. But on his return he falls to his knees before Jesus and addresses him no longer as rabbi but as κύριε; in other words, he addresses him as God. Peter had traversed the path from rabbi to Lord, from teacher to the Son. After this inward journey he is ready and able to receive his calling.

Here we are struck by the parallels with John 1:35-42, the first account in the fourth gospel of the calling of the disciples.[2] There we are told how the first two disciples – Andrew and someone else unnamed – attach themselves to Jesus as a result of being struck by John the Baptist's remark: 'Behold, the Lamb of God.' They are struck on the one hand by awareness of their sinfulness that is echoed in this saying and on the other by the hope that the Lamb of God is for the sinner. We can detect how the two are still uncertain: their discipleship is still hesitant. They follow him cautiously without saying anything; apparently they do not yet dare to address him. So he turns to them and asks: 'What are you looking for?' Their answer still sounds awkward, a little shy and embarrassed, but it is precisely in this way that it leads to what is

---

[2] For the following remarks on John 1:35-42 I am indebted to the stimulating ideas of C.M. Martini, *Damit ihr Frieden habt. Geistliches Leben nach dem Johannesevangelium,* Freiburg im Breisgau, 1986, pp. 204-209.

essential: 'Rabbi, where are you living?' or, to translate it more precisely, 'where are you staying?' Where do you stay, where is the place that you stay, where is what is really you so that we may come there? In this we must remember that talk of staying is one of the characteristic terms of St John's gospel.

We normally translate Jesus's answer as: 'Come and see.' More correctly it should be: 'Come, and you will see.' This also corresponds to the conclusion of the second account of the calling of the disciples, that of Nathanael, where Jesus says at the end: 'You shall see greater things than these' (Jn 1:50). Becoming someone who sees is therefore the content of coming; to come is to enter into being seen by him and seeing with him. Above his abode heaven is open, God's hidden space (cf. Jn 1:51): there man stands in God's holiness. 'Come, and you will see' corresponds too to the Church's communion psalm: 'Taste and see that the Lord is good' (Ps 34:8). Coming, and only coming, leads to seeing. Tasting opens the eyes. Just as once in paradise tasting the forbidden fruit opened people's eyes but disastrously, so here the reverse applies that tasting what is true opens the eyes so that one sees God's goodness. It is only in coming, in Jesus's abode, that seeing takes place. Without daring to come there can be no seeing. John notes that 'it was about the tenth hour' (Jn 1:39); in other words, it was very late, a time when one does not really expect to be able to start anything, and yet a time when what was urgent and decisive took place. According to some apocalyptic reckonings this counted as the hour of the last days.[3] Anyone who comes to Jesus enters into what is final, into the last days: he or she comes into contact with the parousia, the reality of the resurrection and the kingdom of God that is already present.

It is in coming therefore that seeing happens. This is made clear in John's gospel in the same way that we earlier found in Luke's. When Jesus first spoke to them the two addressed him as 'Rabbi'. When they return from staying with him Andrew says to his brother Simon: 'We have found the Messiah' (Jn 1:41). By coming to Jesus, staying with him, he has traversed the path from rabbi to Christ, learned to see the Messiah in the teacher; and it is only by staying with Jesus that one learns this. So the inner unity between the third and fourth gospels becomes visible. Both times people dare to go with Jesus the first time he speaks to them. Both times the experiment of living by his word is

---

[3] Cf. Martini, *op. cit.*, p. 207.

undertaken. Both times there takes place that inward journey that lets seeing arise from coming.

All of us have admittedly begun our journey with the Church's full acknowledgement of the Son of God, but this kind of going off to his abode is for us too the precondition for our own seeing. And it is only someone who sees himself or herself and does not any longer merely believe at second hand who can call others. This coming, this venturing on his word, is also today and always the imperative condition for the apostolate of calling people to the priestly ministry. Again and again we shall need to ask him: 'Where are you staying?' Again and again it will be necessary to go inwardly towards Jesus's abode. Again and again we shall have to cast our nets at his word, even when it seems foolish. Again and again it is a question of regarding his word as more real than that which alone counts as real for us: statistics, technology, public opinion. Often it will seem to us as if it is really already the tenth hour and we must put off the hour of Jesus. But it is precisely in this way that it can be the hour of his presence.

There are still a couple of other features that the two stories share in common. In John the two disciples respond to the saying about the Lamb of God. They have clearly experienced and are aware that they are sinners. And for them this is not some distant kind of religious language but something that churns them up inside, that means reality for them. Because they know this, the Lamb represents hope for them, and for that reason they begin to follow him. When Peter returns with the wealth of fish he has caught something quite unexpected happens. Instead of falling on Jesus's neck because things have turned out so splendidly, as one might expect, he falls at his feet. He does not cling to him to have a guarantee of success in the future but pushes him away because he is afraid of the power of God: 'Depart from me, for I am a sinful man' (Lk 5:8). When God is experienced man recognizes his or her sinfulness, and it is only when he or she really perceives and recognizes this that he or she really knows himself or herself. But in this way he or she becomes genuine. It is only when someone knows that he or she is sinful and has grasped the enormity of sin that he or she also understands the summons: 'Repent, and believe in the gospel' (Mk 1:15). Without repentance, without conversion one does not reach Jesus, one does not reach the gospel. This relationship is aptly summed up by a paradoxical saying of Chesterton's on how one recognizes a saint: 'A saint is a man who knows that he is a sinner.'[4] The fading of the experience of God is shown today in the disappearance of the experience of sin, and the reverse is true: the disappearance of this knowledge distances people from God. Without sliding back into a false discipline of fear we should relearn the truth of the saying: *Initium sapientiae timor Domini,* 'the fear of the Lord is the beginning of wisdom' (Ps 111:10). Wisdom, real understanding, begins with the right fear of the Lord. We must learn this again in order also to learn true love and to grasp what it means that we can love him and that he loves us. This experience of Peter, of Andrew, and of John is also therefore a fundamental precondition for the apostolate and thus for the priesthood. Only someone who himself or herself has been moved by its necessity and has thus grasped the greatness of grace can preach conversion, the first word of Christianity.

In the fundamental elements of the spiritual path of the apostolate that are becoming visible here what also emerges is the funda-

---

[4] Quoted by Cardinal Suenens, *Renewal and the powers of darkness,* London, 1983, p. 58; on the question, cf. the whole of Suenens' chapter as well as K. Hemmerle, *Das Haus des barmherzigen Vaters,* Freiburg, 1983, pp. 17-25.

mental sacramental connection of the Church and the priestly ministry in general. If baptism and confession correspond to the experience of sin, then the mystery of the eucharist corresponds to coming and seeing, going to Jesus's abode. In a sense that previously could not even be guessed at, it is Jesus's abode with us. 'There you will see' – the eucharist is where the promise to Nathanael is valid that we shall be able to see heaven opened and the angels of God ascending and descending (cf. Jn 1:51). Jesus resides and 'stays' in the sacrifice, in the act of love with which he makes himself over to the Father and through his vicarious love gives us too back to him. The communion psalm 34(33) which talks of tasting and seeing also includes the verse: 'Come ye to him, and be enlightened' (Ps 33:6 Douai). To communicate with Christ is to communicate with the true light that enlightens every man that comes into this world (cf. Jn 1:9).[5]

---

[5] The RSV, following the Hebrew, has translated Psalm 34:5 as follows: 'Look to him, and be radiant' whereas the Vulgate followed the Septuagint and says: 'Come ye to him and be enlightened' (Ps 33:6 Douai). This 'be enlightened' *(illuminamini)* aroused a tremendous echo in the philosophy and theology of the Fathers; to the extent that in its Septuagint form one can reckon this verse to be among the core phrases of the Christian liturgy and theology. Here the question naturally arises of the proper status of the Greek Old Testament,

Let us now consider yet another point shared by the two stories we are concerned with. The enormous catch of fishes tears the nets. Peter and those with him cannot reach the bank. They beckoned their companions in the other boat to come and give them a hand. These did so, and they filled both boats so that they almost sank (cf. Lk 5:17). Jesus's summons is at the same time a calling together, a call to συλλαβέσθαι, to use the term in the Greek original, to give each other a hand, to stand together and help each other, to unite the two boats. The same thing is expressed once again in John. Returning from meeting Jesus Andrew cannot keep his discovery hidden. He calls his brother Simon to Jesus, and similarly Philip calls Nathanael (cf. Jn 1:41-45). Being called leads to co-operation. It places people in the body of disciples and demands to be handed on. Every vocation also includes a human element: the element of fraternity, of being aroused by someone else. If we reflect on our own path, then everyone is aware that God's shaft of light-

---

something that needs fresh consideration. Worth taking note of on this is H. Gese, *Zur biblischen Theologie,* Munich, 1977, pp. 9-30, especially pp. 27ff., and cf. also P. Benoit, *Exégèse et Théologie,* vol. I, Paris, 1961, pp. 3-12.

ning did not strike him or her directly but that somewhere there must have been an instance of being addressed by someone who believed, of being carried by someone else. A vocation can of course only endure if we believe not just at second hand 'because so and so has said so' but if we, led by our brethren, find Jesus ourselves (cf. Jn 4:42). Both belong imperatively to each other: leading, addressing, taking along with one as well as one's own 'coming and seeing'. In my view we should therefore once again develop much more courage to address each other and not despise responding to another's witness. This mutuality belongs to the humanity of faith. It is the one component of it. In it one's own encounter with Jesus must mature. Just like leading someone and taking them along with one, so too letting people go and releasing them into the individuality of their own particular vocation is important, even if the individuality appears other than we had thought proper for the person concerned.

With Luke these insights are broadened out into an entire vision of the Church. The sons of Zebedee, James and John, are described there as Simon's κοίνωνοι – his partners is how we must translate it. This means that the three are represented as a small fishing company, as a co-operative with Peter as the boss and chief proprietor.[6] Jesus calls first of all this group, the κοινωνία (fellowship), Simon's co-operative. But in the words with which he calls them Simon's secular calling is transformed into an image of the new thing that is to come. From the fishing co-operative emerges the fellowship, the communion of Jesus. The Christians will form the fellowship of this fishing boat, united by the call of Jesus, united in the miracle of grace that sends the wealth of the sea after the nights without hope. United in what they receive they are united too in their mission.

In Jerome we find an excellent interpretation of the saying about becoming a fisher of men which belongs here, in this inward transformation of Peter's calling into a vision of what is to come.[7] Jerome says that to draw fish out of the water means to tear them away from their vital element and to abandon them to death. But to draw men and women out of the water of the world means to draw them out of the element of death and out of the total darkness of night and to give them the air of heaven to breathe and its light to see by. It

---

6 Cf. F. Hauck, s.v. κοινωνός, in: Gerhard Kittel, *Theological Dictionary of the New Testament,* vol. III, Grand Rapids, Michigan, 1965, pp. 797-809, especially pp. 798-9, 801-2, 804.
7 Jerome, *In psalmum 141 ad neophytos,* CChr 78, pp. 543-544.

means moving them into the element of life that is at the same time light and grants vision of the truth. Light is life, since the human element whereby men and women live most profoundly is truth that is at the same time love. The person who is swimming in the water of the world does not of course know this. Hence he or she resists being drawn out of the water. He or she as it were thinks he or she is an ordinary fish who must die when taken out of the water of the deeps. In fact that is an occurrence of death. But this death leads to the true life in which men and women first really come to be themselves. To be a disciple means to let oneself be caught by Jesus, by the mysterious fish who has descended into the water of the world, the water of death; who has himself turned into a fish so that he can first of all be caught by us, so that he can become the bread of life for us. He lets himself be caught so that we shall be caught by him and find the courage to let ourselves be drawn with him out of the waters of what we are used to and find comfortable. Jesus became a fisher of men by himself taking on himself the night of the sea and himself descending into the suffering of the depths. One can only become a fisher of men if like him one surrenders to this. But one can also only do so if one can depend on

Peter's boat, if one has oneself entered into the fellowship of Peter. A vocation is no private matter, no following Jesus's cause on one's own account. Its context is the entire Church, which can only exist in fellowship with Peter and thus with the apostles of Jesus Christ.

2. Priestly spirituality in Psalm 16

Because the unity of the two testaments matters a lot to me, I would like as my second scriptural passage to deal with an Old Testament text, Psalm 16 (or 15 in the Greek enumeration). The older ones among us will have recited the fifth verse of this psalm when we received the tonsure, when we joined the clergy, as it were as a slogan of what we were then undertaking. Whenever this psalm occurs (it is now the psalm for Compline or Night Prayer on Thursdays) I always have to reflect on how on that occasion I tried in understanding this passage also to understand the process I was embarking on so as to be able to implement it with understanding. In this way this verse has become for me a precious light and remains until today a motto for what being a priest means and how it is realized in practice. In the Vulgate this verse runs: *Dominus pars hereditatis meae et calicis mei. Tu es qui restitues hereditatem meam mihi.* 'The Lord is the portion of my inheritance and of my cup: it is thou that wilt restore my inheritance to me' (Douai).

This verse makes actual what was previously said in verse 1: 'I have no good apart from thee.' It does this in what really is very secular language, in a very pragmatic context that does not yet look at all theological, in other words in terms of land ownership and the division of the land in Israel as portrayed in the book of Joshua and in the Pentateuch.[8] The tribe of Levi, the tribe of priests, remained excluded from this division of the land. It received no land. 'The Lord is his inheritance' (Deut 10:9; Josh 13:4) is what applied to it. 'I [the Lord] am your portion and your inheritance' (Num 18:20). What is involved is first of all a quite down-to-earth system of regulating people's livelihood. The Israelites live from the land that is handed over to them; the land is the physical basis of their existence. The individual is as it were apportioned his or her life through land ownership. The priests alone do not gain their livelihood from working their own land as peasant farmers; the only and indeed physical basis of their life is

---

[8] On what follows cf. H.J. Kraus, *Psalmen,* vol. I, Neukirchen/Vluyn, 1960, pp. 118-127.

Yahweh himself. To put it in actual terms, they live on their share in the sacrifices and on occasional cultic offerings – on what is made over to God and in which they, as the conductors of worship, are given a share.

So here are expressed first of all two modes of physical livelihood which however necessarily lead, on the basis of Israel's thought as a whole, to a greater profundity. The land is indeed for the people of Israel not just a guarantee of maintenance; it is the way in which it obtains a share in the promise God gave to Abraham, its being interwoven into the life of the chosen people that comes from God. Thus at the same time it becomes a guarantee of sharing in God's own power of life. The Levite by contrast remains the landless one, and in this sense the one who is not rescued or provided for, the one outside earthly guarantees. Directly and uniquely he is thrown into dependence on Yahweh alone and immediately, as we are told in Psalm 22 (verse 11). If in the case of land ownership the guarantee of life is somehow at least superficially backed by God and as it were offers an independent form of security, this is not possible in the Levitical form of life. God alone is quite directly the guarantee of life; even earthly, physical life depends on him. If the worship of God existed no longer the foundations for life would disappear. So the life of the Levite is at one and the same time a privilege and a risk. The presence of God in the sanctuary is the only and immediate place of life.

Here an additional comment seems important to me. The terminology of verses 5 and 6 is quite clearly the terminology of the taking of the land and the quite different provision for livelihood that applied to the tribe of Levi. This means that this psalm is the hymn of a priest who is expressing in it the physical and spiritual core of his life. The person who is praying in it has not just interpreted what is provided by the law, the external lack of possessions and living from and for worship, in the sense of a particular type of livelihood, but has lived it on its true foundations. He has spiritualized the law and transcended it in the direction of Christ precisely while realizing its actual content. What is important for us about this psalm is therefore on the one hand that it is a priestly prayer and on the other that here we can perceive the Old Testament's inward self-transcendence in the direction of Christ, the Old Covenant's approach to the New, and thus the unity of the history of our salvation. To live not from possessions but from worship means for this person praying to live in God's presence, to establish one's existence in inward approach to him. On this Hans-Joachim Kraus comments rightly that here the Old Testament allows us to perceive the first hints of a mystical community with God which develops from the particular nature of the Levitical prerogatives.[9] Yahweh has thus become the 'land' of the person praying. How this actually appears in everyday life becomes visible in the next verses. There we read: 'I keep the Lord always before me' (v. 8). The psalmist accordingly lives in the presence of God; he places himself continually before his face. The next phrase varies the same thought when it says: 'because he is at my right hand.' To go with God, to know he is at one's side, to be in his company, to look on him and let oneself be looked on by him – this is seen to be the inner content of these Levitical pre-rogatives. In this way God really becomes the land, the country of one's own life. In this way we live and 'stay' with him. Here the psalm comes into contact with what we discovered earlier in John. To be a priest thus means to come to him, in his abode, and thus to learn to see: to abide in his abode.

How this happens becomes even more comprehensible in the next two verses. The psalmist here praises Yahweh for having coun-

---

[9] *Op. cit.,* p. 123.

selled him and thanks him for having 'educated' him at night. With this term the Septuagint and Vulgate are clearly thinking of the physical pain that 'educates' people. Education is understood as a process of being made straight for being truly human, a process that does not take place without suffering. The term education is intended to be a comprehensive expression for people being led into salvation, for that process of transformation in which from clay we become the image of God and thus for ever capable of God. The outward rod of the disciplinarian is here replaced by the suffering of life in which God leads us and brings us to live with him. All this then also recalls the great psalm of God's word, Psalm 119, which we now recite section by section at Prayer during the Day through the week. It is constructed around the fundamental statement of the Levite's existence: 'The Lord is my portion' (Ps 119:57; cf. v. 14). In this way we find returning in a variety of transformations the themes with which Psalm 16 expounds this reality: 'Their testimonies… are my counsellors' (v. 24). 'It is good for me that I was afflicted, that I might learn thy statutes' (v. 71). 'I know… that in faithfulness thou hast afflicted me' (v. 75). It is in this way that one comes to understand the cryptic message of the prayer that runs like a refrain through the psalm: 'Teach me thy statutes' (vv. 12, 26, 29, 33, 64). When life is in this way genuinely established in God's word what happens is that the Lord 'counsels' us. The word of the Bible is no longer some general and distant text but speaks immediately to me in my life. It comes out of the distance of history and becomes a personal word for me. 'The Lord counsels me': my life now becomes itself a word from him. In this way this becomes true: 'Thou dost show me the path of life' (Ps 16:11). Life ceases to be a dark riddle. We see how it goes. Living opens up, and in the middle of all the tribulation of 'being educated' it becomes joy. 'Thy statutes have been my songs', says Psalm 119 (v. 54), and here in Psalm 16 we find nothing different: 'Therefore my heart is glad, and my soul rejoices' (v. 9); 'in thy presence there is fullness of joy, in thy right hand are pleasures for evermore' (v. 11).

When the Old Testament is read in this way in its core and God's word is accepted as the land of life, then there automatically comes about contact with him whom we believe in as God's living word. It seems to me that it is no accident that in the early Church this psalm became the great prophecy of the resurrection, the portrayal of the new David and definitive priest Jesus Christ. To learn life does not mean to learn some technique but to transcend death. The mystery of Jesus Christ, his death and his resurrection light up when the suffering of the word and its indestructible life-force become experience.

Hence there is no need here for any more great application of this to our own spirituality. A fundamental part of being a priest is something like the Levite's exposure, his landlessness, his being thrown into dependence on God. It is not in vain that the story of the calling of the disciples in Luke 5:1-11 which we began by considering concludes with the words: 'They left everything and followed him' (v. 11). Without an act of leaving of this kind there is no priesthood. The call to discipleship is not possible without this sign of freedom and uncompromisingness. It is my view that it is on this basis that celibacy obtains its great significance and indeed its imperative nature as leaving an earthly future and one's own family life so that the fundamental state of being abandoned to God continues to exist and becomes actual. This of course means that celibacy makes a claim on the whole manner in which we shape our lives. It cannot fulfil its meaning if in everything else we follow the rules of the game of possession that are current in life today. Above all it cannot endure if we do not positively make the core of our life establishing our-selves with God. Just like Psalm 119, Psalm 16 is an emphatic indication of the necessity of continually contemplating and living with the word of God, which only in this way can become our home. The community aspect of liturgical piety that necessarily belongs to this becomes apparent when Psalm 16 talks of the Lord as 'my cup' (v. 5). According to Old Testament usage this reference will be to the festal cup which circulated at the ritual meal or to the cup of fate, the cup of wrath or sal-vation.[10] The priest of the New Covenant praying this psalm can find expressed in this in a particular way that cup through which the Lord has most profoundly become our land: the eucharistic cup in which he distributes himself to us as our life. In this way the priestly life in the presence of God becomes actual as life in the eucharistic mystery. At the profoundest level the eucharist is the land that has become our portion and lot and of which we can say: 'The lines have fallen for me in pleasant places; yea, I have a goodly heritage' (v. 6).

Here there are two comments of a funda-mental kind which still have to be made.

---

[10] Cf. H. Gross and H. Reinelt, *Das Buch der Psalmen,* vol. I, Düsseldorf, 1978, pp. 88-89.

3. Two fundamental conclusions from the biblical texts

(a) The unity of the two testaments

I regard as particularly important in this priestly prayer of the old and the new covenant the fact that here the inner unity of the two testaments, the unity of biblical spirituality and the fundamental ways in which it is lived out in practice, becomes visible and livable. The reason why this is so significant is that a main reason for the crisis of the image of the priesthood that has its roots in exegesis and theology was the separation of the Old Testament from the New, with their relationship coming to be seen only in the dialectical tension and opposition of law and gospel. It was taken for granted that the New Testament ministries had absolutely nothing to do with the offices of the Old Testament. Indeed, the unimpeachable refutation of the Catholic idea of priesthood seemed to be the fact that this could be represented as a relapse into Old Testament ways. Christology, it was said, meant the final and definitive transcending of all priesthood, the abolition of the boundaries between sacred and profane, and also the turning away from the entire history of religion in its various forms and their idea of priesthood. Whenever in the Church's image of the priesthood links could be established with the Old Testament or with the heritage of other religions this counted as a sign that the Church was failing to bring out what was specifically Christian and as an argument against the Church's image of the priest. This meant one was in general cut off from the entire source of biblical piety and human experience and banished to a secularity whose rigid Christomonism had in reality also eroded the Bible's image of Christ. This once again was connected with the way in which the Old Testament itself was envisaged as an opposition of law and prophecy, with law being identified with the ritual and priestly elements and prophecy with criticism of ritual and with a pure ethic of shared humanity that found God not in the temple but in one's neighbour. At the same time the ritual element could be identified with legality and on the other hand prophetic piety characterized as faith in grace. With all this the locus of the New Testament was then established in opposition to ritual, in shared humanity, and any approach to the priesthood that might be made subsequently was not able, on account of this basic idea, to lead to any viable and convincing result.

This entire network of ideas still needs to

be argued against. Anyone who prays the priestly Psalm 16 with the other psalms related to it, especially Psalm 119, will find one thing become quite obvious: that the fundamental opposition and contrasting of ritual worship and prophecy, of priesthood and prophecy or Christology, quite simply collapses. For this psalm is just as much a priestly as it is a prophetic prayer. In it what is purest and most profound in prophetic piety becomes clear, and does so as priestly piety. Because it is so, it is a Christological text. Because it is so, Christianity in its earliest development understood it as a prayer of Jesus Christ which Christ dedicates to us afresh so that we may pray it afresh with him (cf. Acts 2:25-29). What is expressed prophetically in it is the new priesthood of Jesus Christ, and what becomes clear in it is how priesthood in the new covenant based on Christ continues to exist and must continue to exist in the unity of the entire history of salvation. On the basis of this psalm one can understand that the Lord does not abolish but fulfils the law and has made it over to the Church afresh and has truly transcended it, sublated it in the Hegelian sense, as an expression of grace. The Old Testament belongs to Christ and in Christ to us. It is only in the unity of the two testaments that faith can live.

(b) The sacred and the profane

With this I have already reached my second observation. The reclamation of the Old Testament also entails overcoming the denunciation of the sacred and the mystification of the profane. Of course, Christianity is the leaven and the sacred is not something exclusive and cut off but something dynamic. The priest lives with the command: 'Go therefore and make disciples of all nations' (Mt 28:19). But this dynamic element of mission, this inner openness and breadth of the gospel cannot be translated into the formula: 'Go into the world and yourselves become the world, go into the world and confirm it in its secularity.' The opposite is the case. There is God's holy mystery, the mustard seed of the gospel, which does not collapse with the world but is destined to penetrate the entire world. For this reason we must rediscover the courage for the sacred, the courage to distinguish what is Christian: not in order to fence off but in order to transform, to be really dynamic.

Eugène Ionesco, one of the fathers of the theatre of the absurd, expressed this in a 1975 interview with all the passion of someone of this age of ours who is seeking and thirsting for the truth. I quote a few sentences from this interview: 'The Church does not want to lose its old clientèle; it wants to gain new customers in addition. That produces a kind of secularization that is really pitiful.' 'The world is losing its way, the Church is losing itself in the world, the priests are stupid and mediocre [and he would certainly say precisely the same of the bishops], they are happy just to be ordinary people like all the other mediocre left-wing petty bourgeois. I once heard a priest say in church: "Let us be happy, shake each other's hands... Jesus wishes you a happy, pleasant day." Soon for the communion of bread and wine people will set up a bar and offer sandwiches and Beaujolais. This seems to me to be incredibly stupid, to indicate a total lack of *nous*. Fraternity is neither mediocrity nor fraternization. We need that which is outside and beyond time, for what is religion without the holy? There remains nothing for us, nothing solid, everything is in flux. But meanwhile we need a rock.'[11]

In this context I am reminded of some of the provocative things to be found in Peter Handke's new work *Über die Dörfer:* 'Nobody wants us, and nobody ever wanted us... Our homes are rows of despair set up in the void... It is not the wrong way that we are on but no way at all... How abandoned and

---

[11] E. Ionesco, *Gegengifte,* Munich/Vienna, 1979, pp. 158, 159.

alone mankind is, how abandoned and alone!'[12]

I think that if one listens to these voices of people who are conscious, living, suffering, and loving in the world of today it becomes clear that one cannot serve this world with a kind of twee banality. It needs to be transformed, not confirmed; it needs the radicality of the gospel.

A closing reflection: giving and receiving (cf. Mk 10:28-31)

In conclusion, I would like briefly to touch on yet another text: Mark 10:28-31. It is the passage where Peter says to Jesus: 'Lo, we have left everything and followed you.' Matthew adds the question which clearly underlies this remark: 'What then shall we have?' (Mt 19:27). We have already talked about leaving things. As an element of apostolic, priestly spirituality it is indispensable. Let us therefore turn at once to Jesus's answer, which is astonishing. He does not simply dismiss Peter's question, as one might expect. He does not rebuke Peter because he expects

---

[12] P. Handke, *Über die Dörfer,* Frankfurt am Main, 1981, pp. 94-95.

some reward but agrees with him: 'Truly, I say to you, there is no one who has left house or brothers or sisters or mother or father or children or lands, for my sake and for the gospel, who will not receive a hundredfold now in this time, houses and brothers and sisters and mothers and children and lands, with persecutions, and in the age to come eternal life' (Mk 10:29-30). God is magnanimous, and if we look honestly at our lives we know that he has in fact responded a hundredfold to every act of giving up. He does not let us exceed him in magnanimity. He does not wait for the world to come with his answer but already gives us here and now the hundredfold, even if this world remains thereby a world of persecutions, of suffering, of hardship. St Teresa of Avila reduced this saying of Jesus to the simple formula: 'Even in this life God rewards us a hundredfold.'[13] We must merely have the initial courage to start by giving one thing, like Peter, who set out yet again in the morning at the Lord's word – gives one thing and receives a hundred.

So I think that in all our faintheartedness

---

[13] St Teresa, *Life,* ch. 22:15; *The Complete Works of St Teresa of Jesus,* translated by E. Allison Peers, London, vol. I, p. 143; cf. U.M. Schiffers, *'Gott liebt beherzte Seelen',* in *Pastoralblatt* 34 (1982), p. 294.

we should continually ask the Lord for this courage, for the trust, for the faith that is in it. And we should thank him for those to whom he has given this courage and whom he gives to us as a sign of encouragement in order to invite us to make the leap into the hands of his mercy. Priests' jubilees are such days and occasions of thanksgiving. Not just the archdiocese of Cologne but the entire Catholic Church in Germany and throughout the world thanks God today that he has given our Cardinal Höffner the courage to set out at his word, to give his own. On account of this he has had to endure much hardship, but has also been able to experience the opposite – that the Lord gives back in a wonderful way.

Dear Cardinal, in this way you have become for us a witness of Jesus Christ. We thank you, just as with all our hearts we wish you the ability to go on giving for a long time the much you have to give, and we wish that you will be able to go on receiving afresh the answer of God's inexhaustible goodness.